CULTURES OF THE WORLD®

COLOMBIA

Jill DuBois & Leslie Jermyn

 **Marshall Cavendish**
Benchmark

New York

PICTURE CREDITS
Cover photo: © Craig Duncan
Sheila Brown: 21 • Victor Englebert: 6, 7, 8, 9, 10 (bottom), 11, 12, 15, 17 (both), 19, 23, 29, 30, 31, 32, 33, 35, 36, 38, 40, 47, 51, 52, 53, 58, 60, 64, 65, 66, 70, 71, 73, 75, 76, 78, 80, 86, 87, 88, 92, 94, 99, 100, 101, 103, 104, 107, 108, 110, 111, 112, 113, 114, 115, 117, 118, 121 (top), 122, 126, 129 • Getty Images/Hulton Archive: 46, 48, 49, 81 • Eduardo Gil: 3, 4, 10 (top), 14, 18, 22, 61, 63, 69, 74, 79, 89, 96, 97, 102, 116, 119, 124, 125, 128 • HBL Network Photo Agency: 42, 50 • The Hutchison Library: 5, 26, 43, 95, 106 • John Maier, Jr.: 41, 84 • New York Public Library: 20 • Chip & Rosa Maria Peterson: 98 • South American Pictures: 1, 13, 16, 28, 34, 37, 39, 44, 45, 54, 55, 56, 59, 62, 67, 72, 77, 85, 90, 120, 121 (bottom), 127, 130, 131 • Lesley Thelander: 24, 25 • UPI/Bettmann: 91

ACKNOWLEDGMENTS
With thanks to Virginia Tuma, Ph.D. candidate in Literature, Duke University, for her expert reading of the manuscript.

PRECEDING PAGE
Guambino Indian schoolchildren.

Marshall Cavendish Benchmark
99 White Plains Road
Tarrytown, NY 10591
Website: www.marshallcavendish.us

Originated and designed by Times Editions
An imprint of Marshall Cavendish International (Asia) Private Limited
A member of the Times Publishing Limited

Library of Congress Cataloging-in-Publication Data:
DuBois, Jill, [date]
Colombia / by Jill DuBois, Leslie Jermyn.—2nd ed.
  p. cm.—(Cultures of the world)
Includes bibliographical references and index.
Summary: Presents the geography, history, government, economy, and social life and customs of the country of Colombia, located in the northwestern part of South America.
  ISBN 0-7614-1361-8
  ISBN 9780-7614-1361-5
1. Colombia—Juvenile literature. [1. Colombia.] I. Jermyn, Leslie. II. Title. III.
Cultures of the world (2nd ed.)
F2258.5 .D83 2002
986.1—dc21   2001047264

Printed in China

7 6 5

CONTENTS

INTRODUCTION   5

GEOGRAPHY   7
*Topography • Climate • Fauna • Flora • Mineral
wealth • Cities • Bogotá • Medellín • Cali • Cartagena*

HISTORY   19
*Spanish settlements • Nueva Granada • Independence
• Dictatorship and democracy • La Violencia*

GOVERNMENT   27
*The National Congress • The Judiciary • Voting
and elections*

ECONOMY   31
*The mixed economy • Agriculture • Mining • Energy
production • Transportation • Foreign trade*

ENVIRONMENT   43
*Fascinating creatures • Conservation • Oil in the
Sierra Nevada de Cocuy*

COLOMBIANS   51
Indigenous groups • Social system • Dress

LIFESTYLE   61
*Family life • Compadrazgo • Dating and marriage
• Gender roles • Family roles • The work week • Meetings
and visits • Education • Housing • At home in Bogotá*

RELIGION   75
*Church and State • Other faiths • Individual faith
and practice • Religious holidays • Cathedrals*

The painted walls of this restaurant depict life on the Caribbean coast.

LANGUAGE 81
Nonverbal communication • Greetings • Forms of address • Newspapers

ARTS 87
Historical background • Literature • Art • Architecture • Performing and folk arts

LEISURE 99
Water sports • Mountaineering • Hunting • Bullfights • Betting • Sports in rural areas

FESTIVALS 107
Ferias • Día de Negritos/Fiesta de los Blanquitos • Carnival • Independence of Cartagena

FOOD 117
Food shopping • Mealtimes • Table manners • Foods of Colombia • Regional delicacies • Dining out • Drinking customs

MAP OF COLOMBIA 132

ABOUT THE ECONOMY 135

ABOUT THE CULTURE 137

TIME LINE 138

GLOSSARY 140

FURTHER INFORMATION 141

BIBLIOGRAPHY 142

INDEX 142

There are many ways to transport produce and people to the market-place in rural areas.

INTRODUCTION

FROM THE AWE-INSPIRING ANDES MOUNTAINS to the endless plains in the east and the beautiful Pacific and Caribbean coastlines, Colombia is truly one of nature's treasure chests. Precious jewels and metals are abundant in this country, thanks to its unique and sometimes volatile geology. Since the 1980s, Colombia has become famous around the world for drug smuggling and violence. However, in contrast to the negative stereotype of armed drug lords, Colombians are peace-loving people with diverse ethnicities and cultures. Despite years of civil war, Colombians have maintained their African, Indian, and European heritage, their Spanish language, and their warm disposition. The capital, Bogotá, is still referred to as the "Athens of South America," because of its long tradition of producing great leaders in literature and the arts. This book invites you to learn more about Colombia and its people through an exploration of the country's geography, history, lifestyle, customs, and beliefs.

GEOGRAPHY

COLOMBIA IS THE ONLY COUNTRY in Latin America named after Christopher Columbus, the explorer who "discovered" the Americas. Located in the northwestern part of the South American continent, the country has as its neighbors Panama to the north, Venezuela and Brazil to the east, and Peru and Ecuador to the south. Colombia is the only South American country with coasts on both the Caribbean Sea and the Pacific Ocean. With a total surface area of 439,736 square miles (1,138,910 square km), approximately the combined area of Texas, Oklahoma, and New Mexico, Colombia is the fourth largest country in South America. Colombian territory includes eight islands: Gorgona, Gorgonilla, and Malpelo in the Pacific Ocean; and San Andrés, Providencia, San Bernardo, Islas del Rosario, and Isla Fuerte in the Caribbean Sea.

Left: **The Tairona National Park is an untouched area of jungle at the foot of the Sierra Nevada de Santa Marta, a mountain that drops abruptly into the Caribbean Sea.**

Opposite: **Pastos Knot is the point where the Andes mountain range splits into the three *cordilleras* running down the length of Colombia.**

The Cordillera Occidental is the lowest and least populated of the three mountain ranges.

TOPOGRAPHY

The distinguishing feature of Colombia is the Andean mountain chain in the central and western regions. *Cordilleras* ("kor-deel-LYAH-ras"), or mountain ranges, divide the country down its length. Cordillera Oriental (Eastern Range) is the longest; the massive Cordillera Central, the highest. Cordillera Occidental (Western Range) is close to the frontier with Ecuador. Snow covers the summits of the central and eastern ranges, which also have volcanoes. The country is also divided by river systems. The river basins between the mountain ranges contain Colombia's three most important rivers: Atrato, Sinú, and Magdalena. The Magdalena is historically known as the lifeline of Colombia. The river rises in the Andes, flows northeast some 960 miles (1,538 km) between the central and eastern ranges, and empties into the Caribbean. Though it is full of falls, sandbars, eddies, and sunken rocks, it is channeled so that large vessels can travel as far as Barranquilla on the northern Caribbean coastline. The other two great rivers are the Amazon and the Orinoco.

CLIMATE

Mountains, high plateaus, and cool valleys characterize about half of Colombia's land surface. Since the country is situated on the equator, the climate of its various regions is determined mainly by altitude. The coastal and eastern plains, known as *los llanos* ("lohs LYAH-nos"), are at low altitudes and enjoy a tropical climate. The northernmost area of the Andes mountain chain experiences annual temperatures of 65°F (18°C) to 70°F (21°C). This temperate region is largely devoted to agriculture. Small coffee plantations lie on the craggy hillsides, and houses stand in the less tillable areas.

The cold regions, situated between 6,000 and 9,000 feet (1,829 and 2,743 m) above sea level, experience an average temperature of 53°F (11.7°C). Above 9,000 feet, temperatures drop to below 50°F (10°C). Land this high up is too cold for farming and can only be used for grazing. The snow line begins at about 15,000 feet (4,572 m).

The two coasts of Colombia vary greatly in the amount of rainfall each receives. La Guajira, at the northern tip of the country, is the driest place in Colombia, with an average annual rainfall of only 10 inches (25.4 cm). On the other hand, cities in the department, or state, of Chocó receive an average annual rainfall of nearly 400 inches (1,016 cm).

Deserts feature besides windswept plains, wet rain forests, and snow-capped mountains in this land of contrasts.

Right: **The toucan, with its characteristic bill, is one of the many kinds of bird found in Colombia.**

Below: **The cute *irara* makes its home in the Amazonian forest.**

FAUNA

Tapirs, ocelots, armadillos, and many other exotic animals thrive in the tropical areas of Colombia. Several types of monkey are also found in the rain forests. Some, however, such as the brown-headed spider monkey and Brumback's night monkey, are now threatened species.

Macaws, jacamars, cotingas, toucans, and many other birds with bright and colorful plumage make their nests in Colombia. The country has more than 1,500 species of bird—more than anywhere else in the world. These range from the tiny hummingbird to the large harpy eagle, which eats sloths, monkeys, opossums, and guinea pigs. The graceful Andean condor can also be seen soaring over the mountains of Colombia.

The rivers and their tributaries contain fish and mammals usually found in the open sea, such as stingrays and dolphins. The freshwater fish vary greatly in size, from the tiny guppy and neon tetra to the *arapaima*, also known as *pirarucu*, the largest freshwater fish in the world. Colombia's waters are also home to large schools of flesh-eating piranhas.

FLORA

So much variety in climate enables diverse flora to flourish in Colombia. Some 50,000 species of plant, including around 3,000 types of orchid, grow in the country. Cactus grow in the northern deserts, some reaching 60 feet (18 m) in height. In the central plains are vast woodlands. On the Caribbean coast are mangroves and coconut palms.

Orchids with large, vividly colored flowers form a lush undergrowth in the dense Amazonian forest. This tropical region yields ipecac, quinine, and castor beans, used for medicinal purposes, and fruits like papaya, mango, melon, pineapple, passion fruit, and banana. Rubber, chicle, vanilla, ginger, and sarsaparilla also come from this region. Other kinds of plants, virtually unknown in the United States, such as the *curuba* ("coo-ROO-bah"), *chirimoya* ("che-re-MOH-yah"), *guanabana* ("goo-ah-NAH-ba-nah"), *zapote* ("sah-POH-tay"), and *granadilla* ("grah-nah-DEEL-lyah") are also cultivated in Colombia.

The country's temperate regions produce flowers such as roses, chrysanthemums, and *hortensia*, which bloom throughout the year. Coffee plantations are located on the moutain slopes, and various small trees are planted to shade the coffee bushes. Eucalyptus, originally imported from Australia, grows well in the temperate regions. The windy, cold *páramos* ("PAH-rah-mos"), or high plains, of the *tierra fría* ("tee-ERR-rah FREE-ah") are covered with low vegetation of vine shrubs, mosses, and resinous woody plants.

Few plants can withstand the cold winds that sweep across the *páramos*. One that can is the silvery *espeletia*.

The Cauca River winds its way smoothly through the emerald-green sugarcane fields. Thanks to its many rivers, Colombia can depend on hydroelectricity to supply much of its energy requirements.

MINERAL WEALTH

Mineral deposits abound in Colombia. The country is the world's major source of emeralds and ranks fifth in the world in platinum production and ninth in gold. Other significant reserves include petroleum, silver, copper, lead, iron, mercury, nickel, and uranium.

Colombia is also beginning to benefit from one of its most undeveloped regions, the Guajira Peninsula, located on the northeastern corner of Colombia's Caribbean coast. Poor agricultural conditions have prevented the area from being cultivated, although there has been an active salt mine there for years. Recently, however, geologists have discovered that the peninsula is rich in mineral deposits. Unexploited stores of natural gas, coal, and limestone have turned a desert into an economic oasis. The fields of the Guajira Peninsula are currently producing more than 80 percent of the natural gas used in the country's northern coastal region.

Blessed with mountains and rivers, Colombia has become one of the greatest producers of hydroelectricity in Latin America. An ambitious program to develop hydropower is underway. However, supply has still fallen short of demand.

A TOWN OF TROUBLES

It was a quiet night in the central Colombian town of Armero, and most of the 22,000 residents were asleep when the downpour began. But it was not rain that was falling; it was volcanic ash pouring over the whole town. This unusual occurrence in November 1985, marked the beginning of the eruption of Nevado del Ruiz, a volcano in the Cordillera Central that had remained dormant for more than a century. Nobody could have imagined that in the next few frightening hours, Armero would transform from being a home to being a grave for nearly all its citizens.

The roar of destruction echoed through the town, and a formidable torrent of molten mud and rock filled the streets. The eruption of the Arenas crater inside the 18,000-foot (5,486-m) peak melted the mountain's icecap, sending devastating mudslides and floods rushing down into the Chinchina and Lagunilla river valleys.

The eruption of Nevado del Ruiz killed 22,800 people and destroyed 50,000 acres of farmland, 20,000 head of cattle, and 5,000 buildings. The town of Armero was virtually buried under mud, and several smaller local towns were nearly destroyed.

The enormity of the devastation made the grim task of searching for survivors practically impossible. Those who had fled to the hillsides to await evacuation by helicopter were clad in underwear or nightclothes encrusted with mud and covered with blood.

What made the disaster all the more pitiable was that five weeks before the eruption, American and Italian volcanologists had warned Colombian authorities that Nevado del Ruiz, dormant since 1845, was due to come to life soon. Minor eruptions had occurred two months before the catastrophe, and government officials had begun evacuation plans and the plotting of likely paths of mudslides.

But the mountain did not wait.

The capital Bogotá. Colombia's inhospitable terrain has resulted in high concentrations of people in the cities, where settlement is possible.

CITIES

Colombia's largest cities are Bogotá, with a population of 6.1 million; Medellín and Cali, with two million citizens each; and Barranquilla, with one million. Other large cities are Cartagena, Bucaramanga, Cúcuta, Manizales, Pereira, Santa Marta, and Ibagué. Many Colombian cities have grown rapidly in recent years. Immigration from rural areas has raised the country's urban population to 72 percent of the total population. The number of large cities in Colombia is uncharacteristic of Latin America. The capital and two or three other cities usually account for most of the urbanization in most Latin American countries.

BOGOTÁ

The full name of Colombia's capital is Santa Fe de Bogotá. The name Bogotá derives from the original Indian name, Bacatá, meaning "beyond the cultivated lands." Like many other cities, Bogotá is a sprawling metropolis. It is situated in a high valley called the Sabana de Bogotá, at an altitude of more than 8,500 feet (2,591 m) above sea level.

Bogotá is the artistic, cultural, intellectual, and political center of Colombia. It is also becoming a major industrial center. As one of the oldest cities of the Western Hemisphere, Bogotá is the site of many stately colonial churches, homes, and universities. Colombia's capital is really two cities—Bogotá Viejo (the old city) and Bogotá Nuevo (the new city). In the old quarter, scenic narrow streets lined with balconied buildings spread out from Plaza de Bolívar, the heart of Bogotá Viejo. This is where the first inhabitants lived.

Middle-class inhabitants live in ultra-modern buildings in the northern part of the city, where embassies, large private residences, and exclusive boutiques are also located. The broad boulevards, modern skyscrapers, and shopping centers of Bogotá Nuevo create a stark contrast to the historical architecture of Bogotá Viejo. Working-class neighborhoods are in the southern and western areas of the city, where industrial plants are also located.

Bogotá is the focal point of all political, economic, and cultural activity in Colombia.

Bogotá has many museums tracing various aspects of Colombian art and history. The Colonial Museum has paintings of the Spanish colonial period. Handicrafts are exhibited at the Museum of Popular Arts and Traditions. Works done by the Indians of San Agustín are displayed at the National Museum. The Museo del Oro contains more than 25,000 gold objects, the world's largest collection of pre-Colombian goldsmiths' work.

As in other Colombian cities, streets in Bogotá run in straight lines and are called *carreras* ("kar-REH-ras") when running east to west and *calles* ("KAHL-lyes") when running north to south. The migration of people from the countryside has created *tugurios* ("toor-GOO-ree-os"), or slums. As in many other major cities, unemployment, poverty, and crime are common problems.

MEDELLÍN

Colombia's second largest city is Medellín, known for its textile industry. In recent years, it has become famous for being home to one of the largest cocaine-selling cartels. Just outside Medellín is El Ranchito, one of the world's outstanding collections of orchids.

Medellín was founded in 1616. Spaniards looking for opportunities to mine Medellín's gold deposits began settling there in the late 1600s. Many Colombians in Medellín today are descendants of these settlers. As the mines gave out, the early inhabitants quickly became proficient farmers. The region has become the leading coffee-growing area in the country.

Above: **Medellín has overcome the handicaps of physical isolation and rugged terrain to develop into a flourishing city.**

Opposite, top: **The Plaza de Caicedo Cathedral is a striking example of Cali's colonial architecture.**

Opposite, bottom: **Cartagena, an old fortress city located on the Caribbean coast. The old and new harbors face each other.**

Called the "City of Eternal Spring," Medellín has an agreeable climate and a dramatic mountain vista. There is a feeling of growth and prosperity about the city, which boasts many modern hotels, banks, offices, shops, and skyscrapers. Its flower-lined avenues are a pleasant surprise to visitors expecting to see the smokestacks of an industrial city. Medellín's bustling community is host to many flower festivals and exhibitions, and bullfights are a favorite pastime of the citizenry. On weekends during bullfighting season, La Macarena, a 10,000-seat bullring, is the center of much enthusiasm.

CALI

Founded in 1536, Cali is another of Colombia's old cities. This city has undergone exceptional growth over the last two decades, but many colonial buildings still stand. Cali is a manufacturing and distribution center that lies on the edge of Cauca, the country's vital agricultural valley.

The valley is responsible for 20 percent of Colombia's industrial output, comprised mostly of paper and sugar production. In spite of Cali's commercial focus, cultural and sporting endeavors are still popular. Many sporting contests and art exhibitions are held in the city.

At an altitude of 3,300 feet (1,006 m), Cali has a pleasant climate all year, with significant rainfall during its two rainy seasons. Flooding is a problem in lower sections of the city, and several earthquakes have hit Cali in the past few years. Some of Colombia's most hopeless slums are in Cali. In the past, dirt, disease, and poverty caused half the city's children to die before reaching the age of five.

CARTAGENA

Cartagena is one of the most picturesque towns in South America and has some of the finest examples of 16th-century architecture in the Western Hemisphere. In its early days, Cartagena was the most important fortified city of the Spanish Empire, and much of the fortification remains today. Sixteen miles (25.7 km) of protective wall surround narrow streets and adobe buildings, providing an exceptional view. On one side is the Caribbean and on the other is the charming old section of the city. The contrast between old and new is prominent. Houses in the new part of Cartagena are of varied styles. Many are brightly-colored two-story homes with attractive gardens, patios, and balconies. Within the old section remain seven fortresses that previously protected the harbor and the city. Street vendors and women carrying trays on their heads preserve the flavor of this picturesque place.

HISTORY

IN 1500, ALFONSO DE OJEDA became the first European to reach the shores of what is now known as Colombia. At that time, the area was inhabited by as many as eight different Indian groups, all of whom spoke different languages. The population at that time was possibly as large as 700,000. The most advanced were the Chibcha, or Muisca, as they called themselves. They were mainly hunters and fishermen, but many lived by working the land and trading, and a good number were goldsmiths.

The coastal Indians proved so hostile that the earliest explorers withdrew quickly. But the exquisite gold ornaments fashioned by the Indians provided such a lure that Spanish explorers spread the word of a land of fabulous treasure—they called it "El Dorado"—and set off for the Americas hoping to bring the treasure back to Spain.

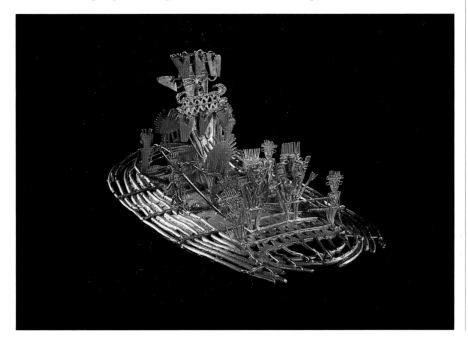

Left: **A replica of the Chibcha "El Dorado" raft is on display in Bogotá's Gold Museum.**

Opposite: **Mysterious ancient stone statues at San Agustín bear witness to Colombia's rich Indian heritage.**

THE LEGEND OF EL DORADO

The Chibcha, or Muisca, believe that a meteor fell to Earth and formed a great crater filled with water. In this lake, which is now called Guatavita, initiation rites were held for Chibcha chieftains. The chieftain's body was rubbed with a glue-like substance and was then covered with gold dust. The golden leader was then rowed to the middle of the lake aboard a raft holding gifts to the gods. On the shore, tribesmen knelt in awe among blazing bonfires. The new chief would then dive into the water and wash the gold dust into the lake as an offering to the deities. The treasures from the raft were added to the lake and the people on the shore added precious items of their own.

This simple Chibcha ceremony was the basis for the legend of El Dorado, a term that now refers to any place where there is enormous wealth. The story inspired the Spanish to launch numerous explorations in search of these riches. The eventual conquest of the Chibcha ushered in Colombia as we know it.

Courtesy of New York Public Library

SPANISH SETTLEMENTS

The first permanent Spanish settlements were made at Santa Marta in 1525 and at Cartagena in 1533. However, the interior of the country was not penetrated until 1536, when Gonzalo Jiménez de Quesada traveled up the Magdalena River. He and his men defeated the Chibcha Indians they encountered in the various mountain valleys and founded the city of Bogotá in 1538.

At about the same time, an expedition from neighboring Ecuador, under the command of Sebastián de Benalcázar, had come up the Cauca valley and founded Pasto, Popayán, and Cali. Another expedition led by Nicolaus de Federmann met up with Benalcázar's group as they both reached Bogotá. This initiated a period of conflict among the various conquering groups.

Rather than fight, however, the three *conquistadores* ("kon-KEES-tah-dor-ehs"), or conquerors, submitted their claims to the court of Spain. Federmann received nothing. Benalcázar was named governor of Popayán, and Jiménez de Quesada was given the military title of marshal and was allowed to remain on the land he had won for Spain. He named the newly conquered land Nueva Granada and its capital, Santa Fe de Bogotá.

In the 15th and 16th centuries, Spain developed into a serious naval power and colonized a large portion of South America.

Cartagena was fortified to defend the country from attacks by English and Dutch pirates who coveted the gold being shipped to Spain.

NUEVA GRANADA

In 1550, a royal government was established for the administration of Colombia. In that same year, gold was discovered in Antioquia. As soon as gold shipments to Spain commenced, English and Dutch pirates began their attacks on Spanish ships and Caribbean ports. However, the interior of the country was able to develop undisturbed.

Despite Nueva Granada's great wealth, Spain was only mildly interested in this territory. For the first 200 years of Spanish rule, the land was governed by a president appointed by the viceroy of Peru.

During this time, however, Cartagena developed as the major port through which all trade with South America was supposed to travel. With the addition of the territory of present-day Ecuador and Venezuela, Colombia became a viceroyalty in its own right in 1739.

The Monument to Independence stands on the site where Bolívar and other patriots won their battle against the colonialists.

INDEPENDENCE

The movement for independence started in the 1790s after the French Revolution. Venezuelans revolted in 1796 and 1806, but an attempt to set up an independent government in Bogotá failed.

In May 1810, Cartagena declared independence. Bogotá followed on July 20, and six years of independence ensued. At that time, Spain was involved in a war against France in Europe, but regained the territory in 1816. Independence finally came in August 1819, when Simón Bolívar and his generals defeated the Spaniards at the Battle of Boyacá.

Bolívar and his generals, however, could not agree on the new form of government. Bolívar preferred a strong central government, while José Antonio Páez and Francisco de Paula Santander pushed for a federation of sovereign states. In 1821, the Constitution of Cúcuta formally set up the federation called the Republic of Colombia, which included Panama, Venezuela, and Ecuador. Present-day Colombia was known as Nueva Granada. It was only in 1863 that it took the name of Colombia. Historians refer to the former federation as Gran Colombia to avoid confusion.

Bolívar was elected president of Gran Colombia, while continuing the fight for Ecuador's liberation and Peru's independence. In his absence, Santander, his vice-president, governed the nation.

DICTATORSHIP AND DEMOCRACY

The federation was doomed from the start. In 1827, Bolívar established a dictatorship, but had to resign in March 1829 because of opposition. Two years later, Santander became president and instituted a democratic state.

By 1849, two political parties were firmly established: the Conservatives, in favor of central government and closely tied with the Catholic Church, and the Liberals, favoring a federation of states and separation of church and state. From 1840 to 1880, the two parties alternated in power, amid much civil strife. But the economy and population prospered, and trade and communications improved.

Poet Raphael Núñez was elected president in 1880. Though a declared Liberal, he held conservative views. Núñez ruled as a dictator until his death in 1894. He made Catholicism the state religion and restored a centralized government.

Meanwhile, the economy experienced little growth, and soon the War of a Thousand Days broke out. More than 100,000 people were killed, and the country was brought to the brink of economic collapse. Shortly after the restoration of peace, Panama seceded with the help of the United States. This interference resulted in bitter Colombian-American relations that lasted for many years.

Simon Bolívar, *El Libertador*, led the revolution which overthrew Spanish rule. His memory is held in great esteem throughout South America.

The period between 1903 and 1930 was unusually stable. Colombia developed a vigorous foreign trade, initially by exporting coffee. Multinational corporations invested in banana and petroleum production. Colombia experienced boom years in the 1920s. Railroads and power plants were built, but the affluence led to over-expansion and inflation.

LA VIOLENCIA

The Great Depression brought financial disaster. In 1930, the government began economic and social reforms. In 1944, a new labor code provided for minimum wages, employee benefits, and trade unions.

After the Second World War, there were severe political crises, resulting in the assassination of popular leader Jorge Eliécer Gaitán in 1948. Thus began "La Violencia." In the next 10 years, 200,000 persons lost their lives. In 1958, a public agreement was reached. Under the accord, the Conservative and Liberal parties agreed to rotate the presidency for 16 years. Each four-year administration ruled over a coalition government.

"La Violencia" from 1948 to 1958 is one of the bloodiest periods in Colombian history.

In recent years, Colombia has experienced the rise of armed guerrillas. At the end of 1985, they united to form Unión Patriótica, which is now represented in the congress. The right-wing groups refused to accept these newly politicized guerrillas, and by the beginning of 1990, over a thousand Union Patriotica officials had been murdered. In June 1998, the Conservative opposition candidate, Andrés Pastrana Arango, son of former President Misael Pastrana Borrero, won the presidential vote in a runoff election. Pastrana has pledged to take a personal role in negotiations with rebel leaders, in an effort to end the civil conflict that has raged for more than three decades and claimed at least 35,000 lives.

GOVERNMENT

COLOMBIA IS A DEMOCRATIC REPUBLIC with a centralized government and separate executive, legislative, and judicial branches. It is a basic structure of national government that is quite similar to that of the United States. It has a long history of democracy, which is quite notable in a continent known for dictatorships.

The president is elected by direct vote for a four-year term and cannot serve more than one term in succession. As chief legislative executive, he has the power to approve or veto legislation. He appoints a cabinet of 13 ministers and is assisted in decision-making by a 10-member consulting body called the Council of State. The president acts as commander-in-chief and directs internal affairs.

THE NATIONAL CONGRESS

The legislative branch is known as the National Congress. It is a bicameral (two-house) congress composed of the Chamber of Representatives and the Senate. Representatives and senators are elected to serve four-year terms. Each department, or state, is represented by two senators-at-large and an additional senator for every 200,000 people. There are two representatives for each department plus an additional one for every 100;000 people. Currently, there are 102 senators and 161 representatives.

Opposite: **Guards on duty at the Government Palace in Bogotá.**

PREAMBLE TO THE CONSTITUTION OF 1886

"In the name of God, supreme source of all authority, and for the purpose of strengthening national unity and securing the benefits of justice, liberty and peace, we have decided to decree, and we do hereby decree, the following POLITICAL CONSTITUTION OF COLOMBIA."

Colombia is a democratic country. The seat of the government is the Congress Building in Bogotá.

THE JUDICIARY

The basic law of Colombia is the constitution of 1886. The system of courts includes a Supreme Court of Justice that tries cases involving interpretation of the constitution and impeachment. It also serves as the final court of appeal. Justices of this court are nominated by the president and elected by the congress. They are reappointed every five years.

Administratively, Colombia is divided into 33 units, including 32 departments and the Distrito Capital de Santa Fe de Bogotá, or Capital District of Bogotá. Governors appointed by the president head each department and are included in the executive branch.

At the local level, mayors of cities are elected by popular vote. Deputies for assemblies of the various department and municipal councils are also chosen by direct vote.

VOTING AND ELECTIONS

Voting is open to all citizens over the age of 18. In August 1957, a special act was passed allowing women to take part in national elections. Colombians must register to vote and have a citizenship card. Voting is considered a legal right but not a duty, and there are no literacy or land ownership requirements. In past elections, participation has been as low as 30 percent. People not allowed to vote include members of the national police, active members of the armed forces, and a small number of people who have lost their political rights by law.

Voter registration takes place at the municipal level, which means that there are local offices to handle the process. Although the requirements for voting are not strict, registration is somewhat complicated, and re-registering after moving to another district is very involved.

Polling places are supervised by a committee made up of two members of each political party. Committees report the results to the municipal registrar, and the results are forwarded to the national registrar.

Colombia's political scene is dominated by two parties, the Liberals and the Conservatives. Elections are always strongly contested.

ECONOMY

ECONOMIC DEVELOPMENT IN COLOMBIA can be divided into four periods. The first ended in 1880, before which time the country had no stable exports to help buy foreign goods.

Coffee paved the way for the second period, which lasted until 1930. Export of this plentiful commodity paid for manufactured goods from abroad. At this time, industry also developed near Medellín.

The third period began during the Great Depression and was marked by industrialization on a national scale. Until 1967, the economic policy of the country stressed industrialization. Revenue from coffee was used to purchase intermediate goods, or materials for factories being developed.

In the present fourth period, the government has encouraged the export of other goods to supplement coffee and refined petroleum, the country's main exports. Supplementary exports have become a reliable source of foreign currency.

Left: **A cotton harvest at Palmira. Agriculture plays an important role in the Colombian economy.**

Opposite: **Ships dock in Barranquilla harbor, Colombia's main port.**

31

THE MIXED ECONOMY

Private enterprise is stronger in Colombia than in most Latin American countries. In fact, one of the most dynamic capitalist projects in Latin America took place around Medellín at the beginning of the 20th century. There was a surge in the growth of industrial plants, especially textile factories. The success of this venture convinced everyone that the government could not manage the economy alone and needed the aid of the private sector.

The government involves itself in the economy in unique ways. The Colombian economy is defined as a mixed economy. There are separate functions for the government, for private home-grown businesses, and for foreign multinational corporations. The government's role is considered essential to lead the nation to full development. The government owns transportation systems, roads, and telecommunications, and it produces and administers the country's electricity. Also, as owner of the subsoil, the administration is expected to develop energy resources. The state is also directly involved in the economy through its control of tariffs, taxation, and exchange rates.

Santa Marta on the Caribbean coast has become a popular tourist resort.

An interesting aspect of the way the private sector operates is that it does not invest in enterprises considered essential to national development. However, when these enterprises become profitable, the government sells them to private corporations.

Colombia's major trading partners are the United States, Germany, Japan, Venezuela, France, and Brazil.

AGRICULTURE

Colombia is primarily an agricultural nation, largely dependent on coffee. Thirty years ago, about half of the population consisted of agriculturalists. Today, less than one-third of the work force is engaged in agriculture. One quarter of the nation's land is used for agriculture, of which about 10 percent is devoted to crop production and the rest is utilized for livestock pasture. Colombia produces a wide range of crops, from bananas, which need warm temperatures, to potatoes, which flourish in a cooler climate. However, many people have to farm on inclines that erode easily, and deforestation in the Andean region is intensifying the erosion problem. Many farms in the highlands are quite small, and the owners rely on simple farming methods. Their traditional ways limit them to subsistence farming, which means that their work produces goods needed by the family, with no significant surplus for sale.

COFFEE Colombia is the world's second largest coffee producer. About one-sixth of all arable land in Colombia is dedicated to producing this crop, the second most profitable export after oil. Because the beans grow best between 4,300 and 6,600 feet (1,311 and 2,012 m), the greatest concentration of coffee farms is near Medellín. Coffee is a labor-intensive crop, and coffee farms are typically small.

Cultivation in the shade and picking by hand contribute to the high quality of Colombian coffee beans.

BANANAS Bananas, another significant export, are grown along the country's Caribbean coast. This crop is believed to earn the farmer the best income return per acre. Foreign multinational corporations were initially involved in banana production. However, private Colombian organizations have also entered the market. As much as 40 percent of the total banana production is consumed domestically.

Another contribution to the Colombian economy is the export of fresh cut flowers, which earns a substantial income.

SUGARCANE Sugarcane, much of which is made into unrefined brown sugar, or *panela* ("pay-NAY-lah"), is planted throughout the warm areas of the nation, especially in the Cauca river valley and on the central Pacific coast.

In contrast to a well-defined growing season in many other sugarcane regions in the world, Colombia's sugarcane harvest continues almost throughout the year. This is due to the constant hot and humid climate in the country's growing regions. Warm days and steady rainfall year in and year out provide permanent employment for Colombian cane cutters.

FLOWERS Fresh cut flowers are another important commodity. This commercial activity is concentrated in the *sabana* ("sah-BAH-nah"), or treeless plain, near Bogotá. It provides employment for about 15,000 people. Colombian flower producers supply carnations, orchids, and other popular flowers for the export market.

Vaqueros herd cattle in the eastern *llanos*, one of the most important cattle-raising regions.

CATTLE Livestock is raised commercially in scattered areas throughout the country, although major concentrations are in the Sabana de Bogotá and the eastern plains.

Beef is the major meat produced in the country. In the early 1980s, the cattle population was estimated at more than 26 million, which means that there were almost as many cows as people.

Recently, however, cattle ranchers have met with a number of problems that have made it difficult for them to increase beef production. Nutritional deficiencies among the cattle are the most troubling of these problems.

FISHING Colombian fishermen catch mainly tuna, shrimp, and several freshwater species. The nation's annual fish catch, most of which comes from coastal fishing, is not as substantial as that of some other Latin American countries, such as Chile and Peru. Many observers believe that Colombia has much unrealized fishing potential. The country's fishing industry is active along the coasts and in the Magdalena river valley. Buenaventura and Tumaco are the main fishing ports.

MINING

Colombia is extremely rich in minerals, having mined gold and emeralds since pre-colonial times. During the colonial period, Colombia was the largest contributor of gold to the Spanish coffers. It continues to be the world's leading producer of emeralds, accounting for 90 percent of global emerald production.

Colombia is also a major South American producer of gold and has the world's largest platinum reserves. Today, Colombia's wealth of minerals includes not only gold, platinum, and emeralds, but also nickel, lead, mercury, manganese, coal, and salt.

The Guajira Peninsula has a valuable deposit of clean-burning coal. Because the coal is near the surface, it is easily mined by open-pit or strip mining techniques. The Colombian government and several industrial firms have spent millions to develop this coal mine, which stores possibly as much as 60 percent of South America's coal reserves.

ENERGY PRODUCTION

The oil wells in the Magdalena river valley have been supplying most of the nation's crude oil since the 1920s. Additional oil deposits have been discovered in numerous other areas, including the basin of the Catatumbo River, in the central Caribbean and Pacific areas, and in the eastern *llanos*.

These finds have led geologists to think that there may be more oil deposits near the Andes. In the mid-1970s, Colombia began importing oil to augment its production. But the nation has now regained its self-sufficiency and has even become a modest exporter of oil.

This oil refinery at Barran-cabermeja is run by the central government, which is responsible for developing the energy resources of the country.

To keep up with its energy demands, Colombia makes use of its waterways. The abundance of rivers, coupled with the high rainfall, have led experts to say that Colombia has one of the greatest hydroelectric potentials in the world. Hydroelectric power facilities are located in the Bogotá-Cali-Medellín area, which is known as the "industrial triangle."

The Cauca Valley Authority is headquartered in Cali. This corporation's focus is flood control, improved farming techniques through irrigation, and development of electrical power. This successful venture tripled Cali's electrical power in its first eight years. Currently, about 75 percent of existing power systems use hydroelectric power, and there is the potential to increase this to 90 percent.

TRANSPORTATION

Topography is a contributing factor to obstacles in transportation. The terrain of the Andes and landslides due to heavy rainfall in the heavily populated highlands make road and rail travel difficult and expensive to develop. In some areas, mules are sometimes the only means of transporting people and goods across the terrain. In more developed spots, aerial cable cars are the main option. Here are other alternatives:

RIVER River travel is very important. In fact, before the railroad from Bogotá to Santa Marta was built, the Magdalena River was the major travel route between the Caribbean coast and the interior. Not too long ago, almost 95 percent of all commercial inland water travel took place on the Magdalena. In times of drought, however, this mode of transportation becomes impossible.

Colombia's uneven landscapes make overland travel rather difficult. Ships play an important role in the transportation industry.

ROAD The country has nearly 68,000 miles (109,435 km) of road, of which only 6,500 miles (10,461 km) is paved. The irregular terrain makes the construction of roads a very costly venture.

There are, however, three important road systems that run north to south between the mountain systems. In addition, the Simón Bolívar Highway, which is 2,300 miles (3701 km) long, runs from Guayaquil in Ecuador, east through Colombia, to Caracas in Venezuela, and a section of the Pan-American Highway connects Bogotá, Cali, and Venezuela.

RAIL The National Railway System network, which is 2,100 miles (3,380 km) long, is almost completely government-owned. Extensive extensions to the railway in the 1940s and 1950s finally connected the highlands with both coasts. The Atlantic rail line was opened in 1961 and runs from Bogotá to Santa Marta. Buenaventura and Bogotá are connected by the Pacific rail line. Freight and passenger railway traffic reached its height in the 1960s, when truck and airline services surpassed rail traffic in popularity.

Cargo that would be moved overland in other countries is transported by air in Colombia, mainly by AVIANCA (Aerovías Nacionales de Colombia).

AVIATION To surmount the difficulties of cross-country travel due to the presence of complex mountain systems, Colombia turned to air travel and became a trailblazer in the field of domestic civil aviation. In 1919, Colombia founded its own airline, AVIANCA, which is now the nation's major international airline. This thriving service flies direct to numerous cities in the United States, Canada, and Europe. El Dorado, Colombia's international airport, is located in Bogotá.

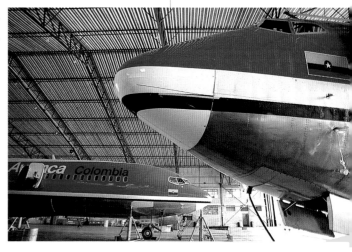

A special technique for washing and drying coffee has enabled the Colombian "milds" to fetch high prices on the world market. Coffee is still a major export.

FOREIGN TRADE

Colombia's imports are mainly raw materials and intermediate goods. Its major exports, as mentioned previously, are coffee, coal, and fuel oil.

The United States and Colombia have long been major trading partners. Prior to 1950, more than 70 percent of Colombia's exports went to the United States, and more than 60 percent of its import activities involved goods from the United States. Currently, 40 percent of Colombian exports go to the United States, and 45 percent of its imports come from there.

New markets have opened in Europe, and Colombia has played a key role in the Andean Common Market. This group's major goal is to reduce trade restrictions among its member nations. Evidence of its success shows in significant trading relationships between Colombia and its neighbors.

WHITE GOLD

Colombia is the heart of the illegal drug trade in South America. Not only does it produce more cocaine than anywhere else in the world, but the city of Medellín is also the control center for most of the export operations to the United States.

The organization and production of cocaine has grown over the decades so that Colombia's drug barons have become extremely wealthy and powerful. At one stage they were known as the "Medellín cartel," because it was believed that as a group, they could fix the price of cocaine and therefore increase their profits. However, there were huge amounts of money to be made and vast areas of land on which to cultivate the coca leaf (unrefined cocaine) so that other growers and traffickers could also participate.

Colossal profits can be made from cocaine even without the operation of a cartel. In any one year, Colombian traffickers earn a total of between $7 and $16 billion from the pure cocaine they provide. In the United States, this has a street value of more than 10 times that amount. Almost all of the money is profit, since there is very little outlay in production. Something like $3 million worth in refining chemicals and coca leaves can make $1 billion in sold cocaine!

This fantastic wealth presents a tempting avenue out of poverty. Colombian peasants who grow coca leaves do not expect to make profits on the same scale as the drug barons make, but can certainly expect to earn three or four times as much from their labor on coca plantations as they would from any other crop.

The Reagan and Bush administrations (1981–1993) in the "war on drugs" campaign found it difficult to halt the expansion of the drug trade for the principal reason that many of the traffickers and workers were too poor to care about prison sentences. They had nothing to lose but their poverty.

The drug barons used their money to gain influence and power in the Colombian government and army and among the people. By doing this, they protected themselves from legal problems. When the United States government wished to have the worst offenders extradited to the United States, immense support from Colombians for the "Extraditables" prevented this.

The amount of money made and the actual quantity of cocaine exported can only be guessed, but authorities on the subject estimate that Colombia produces between 750 and 1,700 tons per year (with a street value of between $83–197 billion), which is something like 80 percent of all cocaine entering the United States. One of the last acts of the Clinton administration (1993–2001) was to approve Plan Colombia, a billion-dollar aid package designed to eradicate drug production in the country.

ENVIRONMENT

COLOMBIA IS A LAND of immense environmental wealth and diversity. This is also a country where issues of the environment are closely tied to politics, economics, and relations with the rest of the world, especially the United States.

As the fourth largest South American country, Colombia has an amazing diversity of plant and animal life. It ranks second to Brazil for having the greatest biodiversity—or variety of plant and animal species—in the world. Colombia is home to more than 1,500 bird species, representing nearly 20 percent of the world total, and around 50,000 plant species, including some 3,000 orchid species.

The reason for this incredible natural wealth is that Colombia has both Atlantic and Pacific coastlines, boasts highlands and lowlands, and experiences tropical, desert, and temperate climates. And finally, its location means that Colombia is home to plants and animals from both South and Central America.

Left: **Yellow highland flowers add color to Colombia's natural landscape.**

Opposite: **Colombia's wild coast is home to some of the country's 50,000 plant species.**

43

The vicuna, a member of the camel family, inhabits certain parts of Colombia.

FASCINATING CREATURES

Colombia's varied ecosystems support a wide range of different animal species. Deserts in the north, grasslands in the east, swamps and wetlands in the northwest, dozens of river habitats throughout the country, and forests ranging from temperate to tropical, broadleaved to coniferous, mountain to coastal, mangroves to coconut palm groves each form a unique micro-environment, which hosts a diversity of plant and animal life, some of which are found nowhere else on earth.

Colombia's animal life includes several species of monkey, wild cat, reptile (such as the Orinoco and American crocodiles), bear, deer, tapir, and armadillo. There are also hundreds of fresh and saltwater fish, including the fabled piranha and electric eel.

Some 1,550 species of bird have been recorded in Colombia—more than the total number of bird species found in the United States and Europe! Colombia's bird life ranges in size from the huge Andean condor that lives in the high mountains to tiny hummingbirds that inhabit the tropical forests.

SYMBOL OF A NATION: THE ANDEAN CONDOR

The Andean condor is Colombia's national animal and the world's largest bird of prey; a fully grown adult weighs an average of 22 pounds (10 kg) and has a wingspan of at least 10 feet (3 m). It can fly 200 miles (322 km) a day at extremely high altitudes when searching for food.

Andean indigenous cultures revered this magnificent bird; in some cultures, killing a condor was a mark of manhood. The condor's habitat once included all of the Andes and the western coastline of South America. Now it is found only in parts of Peru, north and eastern Colombia, northern Venezuela, Patagonia (in the south), Bolivia, and northern Ecuador. The bird has disappeared from much of its former range and is critically endangered where it is still found.

Andean condors are able to reproduce only when they reach seven to eleven years of age. They then mate once every other year and build their nests at altitudes above 10,000 feet (3,000 m). In captivity, safe from human hunters, Andean condors can live as long as 70 years. They feed mainly on dead flesh, but sometimes attack newborn animals and bird colonies as well. Having no voice box, condors cannot make normal bird calls, only wheezes and grunts.

Living in fragile high-altitude environments, the Andean condor leads a vulnerable existence. The expansion of human settlement destroys the bird's habitat. Also, the condor sometimes attacks farm animals, and people hunt it as a pest, if not for its feathers. For the condor population to remain stable, each nesting pair must live long enough for their own offspring to start nesting. This means a lifespan of 25–30 years, which is becoming increasingly difficult for the birds to achieve, as people encroach upon their hunting and foraging grounds.

CONSERVATION

Colombia has set aside approximately 8 percent of its territory for national parks, sanctuaries, and reserves. Examples are Los Flamencos, where pink flamingos stride in coastal lagoons, and Los Estoraques, with its rock formations. But much more needs to be done to protect indigenous flora and fauna. Three animal species have already become extinct, including the monk seal; 19 are considered critically endangered, including the sapphire-bellied hummingbird and Hawksbill turtle; and another 45 are on the endangered list, including the forest falcon, Colombian weasel, giant armadillo, mountain tapir, cotton-top tamarin, and Magdalena River turtle.

Eco-tourism is a major factor influencing conservation efforts. Some of the parks are almost completely undisturbed. Those near cities and along the coasts, however, receive many visitors and need greater care.

The Orinoco crocodile is on Colombia's list of critically endangered animals.

LOS KATIOS: A WORLD HERITAGE SITE

The Los Katios National Park occupies 278 square miles (720 square km) of land in northwestern Colombia, in northern Chocó, between the Atrato River and the border with Panama. The reserve contains several different ecosystems. Some 50 percent of Los Katios consists of lowland swamp forests; tropical rain forest covers the other half of the park, ranging from lowlands to mountainous terrain. The area also includes the floodplain of the Atrato River and the foothills of the Darien mountains in Panama. The Atrato floodplain accounts for 47 percent of Los Katios land; the Darien mountains make up the other 53 percent.

Los Katios merges with the Darien National Park—2,305 square miles (5,970 square km) of land in Panama—to form a massive transfrontier protected zone.

Los Katios was set aside by the government in 1974 and recognized as a World Heritage Site in 1994. A total of 669 plant species have been found in the reserve, 20–25 percent of which are endemic. There are 450 species of birds, representing about 30 percent of all bird species in Colombia, such as the scarlet macaw (*right*). And there are some 550 species of animals in Los Katios, including the manatee, American crocodile, bush dog, giant anteater, and Central American tapir. Los Katios merges with the Darién National Park in Panama, providing a gateway between Central and South America and a habitat for animals from both sides of the border.

Los Katios also protects striking scenery, including the Tendal and Tilupo waterfalls, which measure 82 feet (25 m) and 328 feet (100 m) in height respectively, and the Ciénagas de Tumaradó swamp, home to the manatee.

One of the problems with environmental conservation in this debt and conflict-ridden country is that it often directly conflicts with the need to produce for the world market. The country faces intense pressure from world organizations such as the International Monetary Fund and powerful allies such as the United States to open its territory to a variety of industries. Most of these industries cause environmental degradation by polluting or destroying natural habitats.

A dancer performs in a demonstration against oil exploration in the Sierra Nevada de Cocuy, the land of the U'wa. The Colombian government has granted Occidental Petroleum, an American company, the right to explore the area, in spite of protests from local indigenous peoples.

OIL IN THE SIERRA NEVADA DE COCUY

The Sierra Nevada de Cocuy is home to important ecosystems. Unfortunately, this mountain area also contains oil, the production and export of which Colombia is using to help pay its international debt. Colombia has also agreed to allow the United States, one of its biggest creditors, to explore for oil around the country.

The U'wa, an indigenous people in the area, have fought hard to preserve their dwindling population (only 5,000 left) and shrinking homeland. They believe that oil is the lifeblood of Mother Earth and that to take oil away is to bleed the earth dry.

Although the Sierra Nevada de Cocuy is thought to contain only 1.5 billion barrels of oil (three month's supply for the United States), there seems to be little choice but to sell this resource, if Colombia is to survive financially. This same story plays out all over the country, as nature and human rights are pitted against international pressure and domestic poverty. Saving the environment in Colombia, as in other parts of the world, is a global issue that concerns all of us.

PLAN COLOMBIA: AN ENVIRONMENTAL AND SOCIAL DISASTER

Colombia's unsettled history and unstable economy have led many poor peasants to turn to the cultivation of coca, the key ingredient in cocaine, and poppy, used to make heroine, in order to survive. Since the 1980s, the United States government has been putting pressure on Colombia to eradicate coca and poppy farms, in order to stop the flow of harmful drugs produced from these crops into the United States.

Recently, a new anti-drug aid package worth US$1.3 billion was approved by the United States Congress. Part of this package, called Plan Colombia, includes supplying arms, training, and money to the Colombian military to eradicate drug production once and for all. But the plan has drawn protest from the Colombian people (*below*). One of the primary ways used to destroy drug crops in Colombia is for planes to fly low over the countryside and drop clouds of a herbicide over coca and poppy fields. The herbicide contains a chemical called glyphosate, which kills not only the targeted crops coca and poppy, but also legal food crops and wild flora.

In humans, glyphosate causes nausea, dizziness, vomiting, blurred vision, aching joints, stomachaches, and skin rashes. Furthermore, exposure to glyphosate is believed to contaminate the land in the long term. Ultimately, it is not the rich drug dealers in Colombia or in the United States who suffer, but the natural environment and the poor people of the countryside.

COLOMBIANS

COLOMBIA'S ETHNIC MAKEUP is as diverse as its topography. The population descends mainly from three racial groups: Indian, African, and European, specifically Spanish. Because objective ethnic classification is impossible, the national census ceased reporting population figures by ethnic group in 1919. With no official statistics available, an estimate of the ethnic composition of the population of almost 40 million is: 58 percent *mestizo* ("mes-TEE-soh"), or Indian-Spanish; 20 percent Caucasian; 14 percent *mulatto*; 7 percent African or African-Indian; and 1 percent Indian.

Opposite: **A Medellín girl at the annual flower festival.**

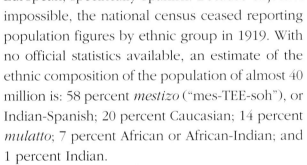

Though ethnic characteristics are important to the people of Colombia, they do not carry the same significance as in the United States. Nonetheless, many Colombians continue to identify themselves according to ancestry and sociocultural status. The various groups are still found in concentrations that reflect patterns set up by the colonial social system. For example, indigenous Indian groups that survived the Spanish conquest are found in scattered clusters, isolated from other ethnic groups, in remote areas such as the Guajira Peninsula. *Mestizos*, who were peasants in earlier times, live mostly in the highlands, where the Spanish *conquistadores* mingled with the indigenous women. In recent years, however, many *mestizos* have migrated to the cities and have become members of the urban working class.

Above: **A *mestizo* man from the Cauca valley. Most Colombians are either Caucasian or *mestizo*.**

Afro-Colombians and mulattos who have not joined the urban migration trend continue to live mainly along the coasts and in the lowlands of the *cordilleras*, where there are few Indians. Caucasians live predominantly in the cities.

INDIGENOUS GROUPS

A variety of indigenous Indian cultures flourished in Colombia before the 16th century and the arrival of the Europeans. The Quimbayas were people inhabiting the western slopes of the Cordillera Central. Skilled craftsmen of this group made elaborate necklaces, rings, breastplates, and nose ornaments. They fashioned these items by pouring molten gold into wax molds. They got their inspiration from nature and shaped their gilded works of art in the form of eagles and owls. Quimbaya craftsmen also made many ornaments from clay.

The Chibchas made up almost one-third of the pre-Columbian population. They called themselves Muisca, but the Spaniards referred to them as Chibcha, which meant "people" in the Muisca language. They lived mainly in the Cundinamarca Basin, which is where Bogotá is today.

The Chibchas developed an advanced and complex civilization. A deeply religious people, they lived in villages and organized themselves along class lines. Each person inherited their rank and status from their mother. To show one's position in society, both men and women often painted their bodies with various designs.

The Chibchas had an efficient system of communal land laws. None of their land was privately owned, and they divided themselves into groups occupying distinct provinces. Each territory was ruled by a local chief, who reported to a more powerful *cacique* ("cah-SEE-kay"), or chieftain. *Caciques* reported to one of the two supreme leaders.

The Chibchas were very skilled in farming, mining, and metalcraft. They grew mainly corn, beans, and potatoes and mined salt, which they traded for other minerals. Although the Chibchas considered salt to be most valuable, they had an immense fortune in emeralds and gold. Many personal valuables were buried with the dead, but fortunately, others have

The indigenous Indian groups west of the Magdalena River were virtually wiped out by the Spaniards. Those that have survived live in small groups and keep to themselves.

Weaving is a traditional craft among indigenous Indians. Here a Cofan woman makes a *mochila* (bag).

survived to the present and can be seen in Bogotá's Museo del Oro.

The indigenous Indian culture in modern Colombia evolved from the Quimbaya, Chibcha, and Carib groups. There are still a good number of indigenous Indian groups, many living in the eastern two-thirds of the country. Some remain isolated, such as the Motilón, who resist all contact with outsiders. This group has been known in recent times to perch in mountain retreats and attack missionary groups or oil company employees with poisoned arrows and blowguns.

Another indigenous Indian group still found practicing a traditional lifestyle in Colombia are the Yagua Indians of the Amazonian jungle. There are approximately 3,000 Yagua Indians, making a living as hunters and fishermen. They live in huts on stilts that protect them from floods brought by torrential rains.

In groups such as the Chimilas and the Sanha of the Sierra Nevada de Santa Marta mountain region, men and boys live in a temple, where they spin cotton and weave cloth, while women and girls live in houses with thatched roofs.

SOCIAL SYSTEM

The structure of Colombian society is based on 16th-century colonial Spanish traditions. At that time, slaves from Africa were introduced to the coastal regions, and the practice continued for the next three centuries. Some slaves were taken to farming and mining regions; others escaped to the interior. Most, however, remained in slavery until its abolition in the mid-1800s.

The Spanish devised a hierarchical society, in which they were the prestigious, wealthy, and powerful. The lower echelons were made up of the slaves and indigenous people. The pattern of settlement left frontier areas and less inhabitable lands to the less fortunate: the non-Caucasians.

Colombian society is still distinguished by its pronounced status differences and limited upward social mobility. But the class system is more flexible in cities than in rural areas. In rural society, there is a rigid structure with few possibilities of upward movement.

The Colombian social system has four divisions: the upper, middle, and lower classes and the masses. The three classes are distinguished by their level of participation in and understanding of the national society. The masses are known for their poverty and illiteracy, which trap them in their powerless position in society. Despite significant economic growth in recent years, poverty remains a problem. Uneven income distribution, with a high concentration of the country's wealth among the economic elite, has contributed to the hierarchical nature of Colombian society.

Other factors that differentiate the classes are lifestyle, education, family background, and occupation. Education is generally considered the key to upward social mobility.

CAUCASIANS Because of the social ranking established during colonial times, fair skin became associated with being Spanish and was therefore considered to be of high status.

Today, Caucasians continue to hold the highest positions in government and business in Colombian society. Having always been a minority in Colombia, Caucasians follow European lifestyles and behavior and the teachings of the Catholic Church. Their artificial sense of superiority influenced the rest of society.

Caucasian Colombians still emphasize the importance of intellectual pursuits, and they encourage genteel and creative activities and professions that are possible for a class who have the time and financial security to enjoy these pursuits.

Careers in business and industry are considered very acceptable for those who are not from the most wealthy and prestigious families. However, the importance of ethnic purity varies from region to region and may not matter as much as an old and respected Spanish surname.

Mestizos **identify with Caucasians and have adopted Western styles of dress.**

The highest concentration of Afro-Colombians and mulattos is in Chocó, where the first Africans arrived.

MESTIZOS Ethnic mixing began in Colombia from the earliest years, and Colombians often refer to themselves as a *mestizo* or mixed nation. Approximately 60 percent of the population is of mixed origin, and these people are found in all social classes, occupations, and regions. One of the most unifying factors within this group is the general perception that the status of *mestizo* or mulatto is better than that of indigenous Indian or Afro-Colombian. Another interesting sociological factor is that *mestizos* are said to identify with the dominant Caucasian group. Mulattos, on the other hand, identify with Afro-Colombians, a self-perception that may make upward social and economic mobility more difficult for them.

AFRO-COLOMBIANS Afro-Colombians reflect the distribution patterns of the colonial period. Most live in the lowland areas on the Pacific and Atlantic coasts and along the Cauca and Magdalena rivers. In Chocó, Afro-Colombians and mulattos represent 80 percent of the population.

The Afro-Colombian groups in Chocó are quite distinctive in their music, marital practices, and funeral rites. Their distinctive music, more than any other element, keeps Chocoan Africans very aware of their identity. Many African Chocoan men are polygamous, which means that they are married to, or live with, more than one woman.

Funeral rites in this region continue for nine days and include nightly prayers, heavy drinking of alcohol, and gambling. These distinctions are cultural remnants of their African slave heritage. Their activities reinforce a sense of identity among the Afro-Colombians in the region.

Few Afro-Colombians have become prominent on the national scene. Many Colombians consider the awful living conditions of Afro-Colombians in Buenaventura a national disgrace.

A SEPARATE PEOPLE

As the Pilgrims crossed the Atlantic Ocean on the *Mayflower* to reach the New World, a sister ship, the *Seaflower*, headed for San Andrés Island. The English Puritans settled on the island. These early settlers were replaced by buccaneers who preyed upon Spanish ships, and later by the Spanish. After the famous English pirate Henry Morgan wrested the island from the Spanish, it remained largely uninhabited for more than 100 years. In fact, in 1780, a visitor from the United States reported that only 12 families were living on San Andrés.

In 1822, the islands of San Andrés and nearby Providencia came under Colombian rule. Since then, they have become a steady supplier of coconut to the United States and a popular vacation spot for Colombians and many North Americans.

Though these glittering islands have belonged to Colombia for more than a century and a half, the inhabitants have so maintained their isolation that they have not even adopted the Spanish language or embraced the national religion, Roman Catholicism. These islanders retain the Protestant religion, continue to speak English, and regard themselves as a distinct group from mainland Colombians.

DRESS

Colombian city dwellers dress in the same styles as people in cities in the United States. Colombian youths are eager to follow fashion trends. They wear *molas* ("MO-las"), or embroidered shirts, as frequently as they wear designer jeans and shirts. Climate influences attire. In warm areas on the Pacific coast, men seldom wear coats. There is often a correlation between the size of the city and the elegance of dress. People in Bogotá have been referred to as *currutacos* ("coo-roo-TAH-kos"), or dandies, in part because of their finery.

Colombians in the countryside sew most of their own clothing. The basic rural garments include the *poncho* ("PON-cho"), *ruana* ("roo-AH-nah"), and *bayetón* ("bah-yay-TOHN"). Each of these garments is a cloak with a hole in the center for the wearer's head to pass through. The garments hang from front to back, leaving the arms free. *Bayetones* are nearly ankle length; *ruanas*, the most commonly worn of the three, are shawls that hang to a little below the waist; and *ponchos* fall between the other two lengths.

Among the poor, *ruanas* are also used as blankets. Woolen *ruanas* are remarkably waterproof because of the natural oils left in the material. The *pañolón* ("PAN-nyah-LOHN") is a traditional women's garment that resembles the *ruana*. The *pañolón* shawl is customarily made from silk or cotton.

Footwear is an indicator of status. Typical shoes are fiber slippers and sandals. Many rural people prefer to work barefoot. In some groups, it is also regarded as ostentatious to wear shoes.

Above: **This Guambino family shows off garments typically worn by indigenous Indians living at high altitudes.**

Opposite: **Ruanas are worn by both men and women and can double as blankets.**

59

LIFESTYLE

LIFESTYLE VARIES BY REGION in Colombia. In Leticia, Colombia's southernmost city, inhabitants depend on trapping and fishing for their livelihood. And even when meeting in the town square, Leticia residents must be wary of the hazards one encounters in the heart of the jungle, for Leticia lies in the Amazonian valley.

On the *llanos*, *vaqueros* ("vah-KAY-ros"), or cowboys, drive their herds all day in the areas where much of the country's meat and cereal is produced. Wearing traditional straw hats, they tether cattle and tend mules, pigs, goats, chickens, sheep, and other livestock.

Fishing villages and harbors thrive along the coasts, where the inhabitants rely on the ocean for their livelihood. Men work on the docks shirtless, loading and unloading cargo with bandannas around their necks.

Above: **In the streets of Colombian towns, like those in other towns in the world, one can see all sorts of people, from well-dressed office workers to street vendors.**

Opposite: **A** *vaquero* **in the** *llanos*, **the cattle-breeding region.**

In the populated areas of the mountains, the numerous coffee plantations are the main income source. Residents there also fish in the clear mountain streams. The typical work day of coffee plantation workers begins at around 8 A.M. They tie a plastic bucket round their waist which they fill with coffee beans. When the bucket is full, they empty it into a plastic sack and start filling it again. The workers move very quickly, because they are paid according to the amount they pick. An experienced coffee picker handles about 110 pounds (50 kg) of beans each day. After working continuously for four hours, the workers take their sacks full of coffee beans to the plantation manager, who measures what has been picked and gives the workers their wages for the day.

City dwellers work city jobs. There are accountants, doctors, lawyers, office staff, janitors, and the like.

FAMILY LIFE

The family is a very important social unit in Colombia. When Colombians refer to the family, they mean a wide circle of kinship consisting of several generations—what a North American would probably think of as the extended family.

The function and structure of the family does vary, though, depending again on regional and socioeconomic factors. Typically, children live with their families until they marry, and often even afterward. Young adults from upper-middle and upper-class families often get their own apartments before marriage, but it is still quite common for newly married couples to live with their large families until they have saved enough money to start their own home.

Family ties are somewhat weaker in urban centers than in rural areas, but households are usually large regardless of locality. Grandparents and other aging relatives are customarily part of the household in addition to the core

The ideal of the family as a close-knit unit is still very much present in all social and ethnic groups in Colombia.

family unit of mother, father, and children. Cousins and their relatives can also join the family circle for extended periods of time when necessary. The set-up is usually flexible. Only the rural upper class has traditional patriarchal domiciles, in which married sons and their families remain in the home.

Sunday is family day. Colombians are likely to visit their families on this day, for the importance of kinship is greatly emphasized. It is the basis of much social and business interaction.

The family also plays a significant role in the Colombian business world. There are many family-run businesses in which few, if any, positions of importance are given to outsiders. Employers feel safe in hiring family members, believing that the relatives' true strengths and weaknesses are well known among the family. In short, there are no surprises from the new employee. Furthermore, a sense of family loyalty motivates employees to keep their boss' best interests at heart.

Among the lower socioeconomic groups, household membership and the structure of the family can be considerably different from those of middle- and upper-class families. The reason for this is that formal marriage may not be the foundation of the family relationship. Sometimes the father is not a permanent resident in the home, and the mother becomes the chief authority in the family. This trend is most prevalent in Chocó, where in the 1960s, about one-third of households were headed by women.

Extended family ties are often weakened in the lower-class family by the ever-increasing need to migrate to urban centers to find employment. But in keeping with Hispanic uniformity in family life, rural migrants will move to areas where other relatives have previously relocated, and the pattern of extended-family living is resumed.

Family background and name are most important to those higher up the social ladder. Colombia's most respected families are descended from 16th-century Spanish settlers. Families with this distinction proudly display crests above the doors of their homes. A sense of pride is kept alive by a tradition of telling stories of the lives and deeds of their ancestors.

Extended families are a feature of Colombian life. In certain regions, households are headed by women, since the men may not always live in the home.

COMPADRAZGO

Kinship ties are stretched even further by a traditional Hispanic relationship known as *compadrazgo* ("kom-pah-DRAHS-go"), a spiritual relationship linked to Catholic notions of baptismal godparenthood. In this relationship, social and emotional bonds are created when a godparent accepts serious responsibilities for a child's welfare, and in turn, earns great respect from the child. Furthermore, a spiritual bond is created between the child's parents and godparents.

While children refer to their godfather and godmother as *padrino* ("pah-DREE-no") and *madrina* ("mah-DREE-nah"), their parents address the godparents as *compadre* ("kom-PAH-dray") and *comadre* ("kom-MAH-dray"), signifying both friendship and companionship and acknowledging the importance of the parent-godparent bond.

Colombians may have several sets of godparents, chosen at various important milestones in their lives. But the baptismal godparents are by far the most important. They often supervise the religious education of the child, and it is not unusual for an orphaned child to be adopted by his or her baptismal godparents.

The godparental relationship is not limited to Colombians of Hispanic descent. Chibcha Indian godparents are involved in rituals such as earlobe piercing, the first clipping of fingernails, and the first cutting of hair. The godfathers who cut the child's hair are said to be the most honored.

Every Colombian has a set of godparents, sometimes several sets, who take a personal interest in their godchild's development through life.

DATING AND MARRIAGE

Dating without chaperones has recently become more common in Colombia, especially among educated families in the cities. Young Colombians develop exclusive relationships rather quickly, and they regard their counterparts in the United States as promiscuous because of the tendency to "play the field."

Most Colombians go through formal marriage ceremonies. However, where indigenous and Afro-Colombian influence is strong, people usually practice trial marriage. Many communities openly acknowledge this as a legitimate prematrimonial stage. Civil marriage has been legal in Colombia since 1973. Before that, only Catholic marriages were valid for Catholics. Nonetheless, many Colombians feel that there is less commitment to civil marriages and thus look down on them. Catholic marriages are viewed as the ideal and as the legal, social, and sexual basis of the family.

Religious marriage also connotes social status, and many Colombians see marriage as a path to social mobility. Parents are always hopeful that their young daughters will marry a man of great status and wealth. But upper-class Colombians are reluctant to wed persons of a lower social status. Matchmaking is not uncommon among the aristocracy, with a second or third cousin often being the chosen match.

Young Colombians at a party.

65

GENDER ROLES

The word "macho" is used a lot in the United States, but its meaning is rarely clear. *Machismo* ("mah-CHEES-mo"), being macho, is actually a Hispanic concept that distinguishes masculine attributes. It provides a guideline for men to follow, and the term does not have the negative connotation it has in the United States.

To Latin Americans, a macho man is one who is strong, respected, protective, and capable of providing for his wife and family. Though aggressiveness is something that North Americans associate with being macho, Colombian men vary in their aggressiveness according to social class. In general, middle- and upper-class men tend to be less aggressive than men in the lower classes.

Colombian women too aspire to a socially-approved image, with much emphasis placed on being feminine. This desired image can be seen in the way Colombian women dress. The women of Bogotá, *bogotanas* ("bog-o-TAN-nas"), dress fashionably even when running errands or just staying around the house. This feminine image is so prevalent that travel guides list the beautiful women of Cali as one of the city's main attractions!

FAMILY ROLES

Many Colombians live with their children, parents, grandparents, and other relatives under one roof, and each family member has a role to play in the extended household.

Traditionally, the father was considered the head of the family, and the mother had full responsibility for preparing meals, doing household chores, and taking care of the children. However, Colombian society is changing, and new family arrangements are arising. The old "macho" man and maternal woman stereotypes are giving way to new gender roles within the modern family. For example, more Colombian women—especially in the middle classes—are finding jobs outside the home and contributing to the family income, while Colombian men are learning to communicate with their children.

Until recently, women of the upper class were not allowed to work outside the home. The only acceptable activity was charitable volunteer work. Even social activities were limited to school and the home, and they were chaperoned at parties. Now, many upper-class women are well educated and enjoy careers in a variety of fields. More legal rights have been granted to women, and their participation and involvement in public affairs, government, and higher education is increasing.

Limitations have always been greater for middle- and lower-class women. It has generally been an economic requirement for these wives to work out in the fields alongside their husbands or to be employed outside the home and contribute their paychecks to the family budget. Unfortunately, wages remain low for these women.

More women are joining the work force. Some even enter traditionally male professions, like this young engineer who works at a refinery.

THE WORK WEEK

Colombians work Monday through Friday and half a day on Saturday. Labor laws prohibit anyone from working more than 48 hours a week.

There are 18 national holidays in Colombia each year, 12 of which are religious. The six secular public holidays are: New Year's Day (January 1), Labor Day (May 1), Independence Day (July 20), Battle of Boyacá (August 7), Columbus Day (October 12), and Independence of Cartagena (November 11). The only day of rest is Sunday.

In the industrial centers, the work day begins between 8 and 8:30 A.M. and ends between 6:30 and 7 P.M. On farms and in the torrid zone, laborers may start work at 6 or 7 A.M.

Government offices are open from 8 A.M. to noon and again from 2 to 6 P.M. Most businesses operate from 9 A.M. to 5 P.M. Monday through Friday. Stores are generally open Monday through Saturday, from 9 A.M. to 12:30 P.M. and then from 2 to 7 P.M., though store hours may vary. Banks open from 9 A.M. to 3 P.M. Monday through Thursday and from 9 A.M. to 3:30 P.M on Friday.

MEETINGS AND VISITS

In Colombia, business appointments are made at least a week in advance, but people may arrive 15 to 20 minutes late for a business meeting.

Colombia has a tradition of hospitality. People often invite friends to their homes. Relatives are the most frequent visitors in Colombian homes. At social gatherings, the host family dresses formally and entertains the guests in the living room.

Supper time ordinarily begins at around 8 P.M., but when there are guests, everyone dines at 10 or 11 P.M. Guests are expected to arrive 15 to 30 minutes late. Drinks and snacks are served before the multi-course dinner begins.

MARKET DAYS

Although rural life involves a lot of hard work, country dwellers do enjoy some recreation. They especially look forward to market days.

One day of the week is designated market day in a village, and people from miles around come to visit and enjoy the festivities. All modes of transportation are employed, not only to bring produce, animals, and handicrafts to the market, but also to transport the visitors. Open-air buses packed with passengers are seen on the road next to *burros* ("BOOR-ros") and push carts.

The marketplace is usually located in the main square of the village. Goods and wares are spread out on wooden stands or stacked on the ground. Chickens strut past as people bargain with their friends and neighbors.

Market days are a great opportunity for people in the countryside to meet one another, catch up, and trade in a variety of goods.

The "classroom" for these Noanama children is an open hut built on stilts in the rain forest.

EDUCATION

Colombia spends very little of the national gross domestic product on education. Nonetheless, free education is available to all, and the adult literacy rate is 91.3 percent.

There is still the perception among Colombians that private education is superior to public education. Wealthier Colombians prefer to send their children to private schools, and it is also common for middle-class children to attend private schools. Schools in Colombia are called either *escuelas* ("es-coo-AY-las") or *colegios* ("co-LAY-he-os").

Despite increases in government spending on education, some problems remain in the public education system. In the countryside, for example, there are sometimes not enough seats available in the schools.

School is compulsory for all Colombian children between the ages of 5 and 16. However, education is not a priority among the poorest families. For them, the money that the children can earn from work is needed to support the household.

ELEMENTARY Free elementary education consists of two years of kindergarten and five years of elementary school. Entrance into high school is dependent on completion of the elementary program.

HIGH SCHOOL High school programs take six years to complete. Students can then be admitted to an institute of higher education.

VOCATIONAL High school programs are assuming a vocational focus. This change is intended to prepare students to meet the country's need for skilled labor in both agriculture and industry. This new emphasis is a real change from previous patterns of education that concentrated on preparing high school students to enter colleges and universities.

Today there is more emphasis on vocational training, such as in fashion design.

COLLEGE More than 320,000 students, some of whom are from the working class, attend 73 universities in Colombia. There are perhaps another 60 additional institutions of higher education in the country.

Because of the challenging terrain and overwhelming poverty, often there is no way for children to get to school, and education by radio and television has been very successful. Colombia was the first South American country to use radio for this purpose. Rural people gather around a radio set up in a public place, and lessons in reading, writing, history, and geography are transmitted over the air waves. Television was added to the rural educational system in the early 1980s in order to reach all areas of the country in a more contemporary and effective manner.

HOUSING

In Leticia at the edge of the Amazonian forest, houses are built on stilts for safety.

Housing in Colombia is designed in different styles and built from different materials, reflecting the climate in the location and the income level of the occupant. Classic colonial mansions and modern ranch-style houses can be found in the cities and suburbs, while on the outskirts stand the most desperate slums, called *tugurios*, where unemployment, poverty, and crime are rampant. In the rural areas, a large ranch of an upper-class family may be located near the small landholding of a subsistence farmer.

In remote areas, people live in bamboo or thatched *tambos* ("TAM-bos"), which are built on stilts that hold the structure about six feet (1.8 m) above the land or water. In swampy areas, the stilts keep the water from getting into the house, and in dry regions, they protect the occupants from snakes, insects, and other dangerous wildlife. One of the stilts is notched to enable the occupants to climb up into the house.

Other rural homes are also very simple and often have no access to electricity or running water.

Until recently, rural housing was generally inferior to urban housing. Heavy rural-to-urban migration by people desperate to make a living and support their families put immense pressure on cities to try to keep up with the demand for new housing.

Medellín's efforts to meet housing needs is further complicated by its position. It faces mountains in nearly every direction and so has no means of spreading out. The housing trend in Medellín and other large cities is toward tall, modern apartment buildings.

In La Candelaria, Bogotá's old section, houses form a solid wall facing the street.

AT HOME IN BOGOTÁ

Houses in Bogotá form a solid wall facing the sidewalk. There are no side yards, and neighbors cannot speak to each other over a fence, because the rear patio is surrounded by a high wall. There are also no back doors.

The home has two floors and no basement. The windows on the first floor are striped by iron bars or ornamental grillwork for security. Most modern homes have a patio in the back. Part of this patio is a garden, usually accessible from the living or dining room.

Most homes also have a maid's quarters with direct access to the kitchen, garage, and service patio. The location of the maid's quarters facilitates her work. Traditionally, the maid is responsible for the first-floor chores—cooking in the kitchen, washing and ironing on the patio, and accepting deliveries through the garage. The señora would tend to the chores upstairs, where the bedrooms and bathrooms are located. She would spend a lot of time upstairs in the bedroom, even entertaining her women friends there. The living room is seldom used, and the family congregates in the upstairs hallway.

RELIGION

THE COLOMBIAN CONSTITUTION guarantees freedom of worship. Nevertheless, some 90 percent of all Colombians are Roman Catholic.

Roman Catholicism has been the established religion in this country since the 1500s. The Church in Colombia is known as one of the most conservative and traditional in Latin America. There has long been a great emphasis in the Catholic Church in Colombia on the formal aspects of the faith, and most Colombians regularly observe holy days, attend Mass, and receive the sacraments.

Catholic churches are the biggest, most imposing buildings in all Colombian towns. The parish church is the center of activity in most communities, and Colombian churches serve some of the largest Mass congregations in Latin America.

Left: **Jesus' triumphant entry into Jerusalem is marked by a procession on Palm Sunday, one week before Easter.**

Opposite: **The San Pedro Claver Church in Cartagena.**

Holy Week processions are an important event in the Catholic Church's calendar.

CHURCH AND STATE

The constitution of 1886 gave special status to the Catholic Church, and the concordat of 1887 between the pope and the Colombian government defined a special role for the Church in civil matters. However, in 1853 Colombia was the first Latin American country to pass a law separating Church and State. The concordat and constitution remained in effect until 1973, when a new concordat was issued. The Church lost its influence in education, in the territories occupied by indigenous Indians, and in marriage regulation. However, the Church still has a profound political influence, and its close alliance with wealthy Conservatives has sparked debate about its traditional role and majority appeal.

OTHER FAITHS

Only 10 percent of the population is divided among Protestants, Jews, Baha'is, Muslims, Buddhists, Hindus, and Indian tribal religionists. There are local Baha'i spiritual assemblies and synagogues for the more than 10,000 Jews in the country. Indian tribal religions are practiced by a number of lowland and jungle groups, including the Arhuaco, Coreguaje, Cuna, Kogua, Guajiro, Macu, Barasano, and Tatuyo.

The First Communion is an important event in a Catholic person's life.

INDIVIDUAL FAITH AND PRACTICE

In 1970, a general survey in Colombia found that 63 percent of Catholics attended Mass at least once a week, 67 percent prayed daily, and only 24 percent did not pray at all. This represented a marked difference from results obtained in 1960, when only 10 percent were said to fulfill these minimum requirements of Catholicism. Since then, there was a resurgence of conservative worship.

Though many people in the urban areas only attend Mass on religious holidays, their beliefs and values remain faithful to religious teachings. Major family events such as birth and baptism, marriage, and death are usually celebrated in church.

RELIGIOUS HOLIDAYS

Of Colombia's 18 national holidays, 12 are religious, specifically Catholic. Easter and Christmas are the most important. The remaining 10 are Epiphany (January 6), St. Joseph's Day (March 19), Maundy Thursday, Good Friday, Corpus Christi, Saints Peter and Paul Day (June 29), Assumption Day (August 15), All Saints Day (November 1), and Immaculate Conception Day (December 8).

The Kogua Indians live in small villages in the Sierra Nevada de Santa Marta.

THE KOGUA TRIBAL RELIGION

The Kogua are Colombian Indians who live on the slopes of the Sierra Nevada de Santa Marta. This farming group of 5,000 treasures its ancestral lore about the laws of nature and the governance of the universe. The Kogua high priest, or Máma, contemplates the skies, because true knowledge for the Kogua is the knowledge of the laws of Mother Nature. For them, living in harmony with these laws is the key to the preservation of the universe.

The high priest is responsible for watching over the universe, as well as watching over the spiritual and social order of the group. He knows the Kogua theory of the nine-stage creation of the universe. This knowledge, combined with the laws of nature, means the Kogua believe that they alone hold the secret of what causes the sun to rise each morning and what determines the way things are born and mature, multiply and die.

CATHEDRALS

There are a number of notable places of worship in Colombia, most dating back to colonial days. One cathedral that is somewhat unusual is in a salt mine in Zipaquirá! It was carved from salt by the miners, and as many as 15,000 people can congregate in its immense gallery. The 75-foot (23-m) high ceiling arches above an 18-ton (18,000-kg) block of salt that is the main altar.

The Church of San Francisco in Popayán has a bell that can be heard throughout the valley. In its pulpit is a gracefully carved figure of a Creole girl carrying a basket of fruit atop her head. The altarpiece carving of the Virgin of the Immaculate Conception is also very impressive. Outside the church stand simple stone carvings in contrast to the intricate carvings within.

Cartagena's cathedral, located in Plaza de Bolívar, has a fortress-like exterior that was completed in the early 1600s. While under construction, the cathedral was partially destroyed by the cannons of Sir Francis Drake, the English seaman and adventurer. Spain and England were at war at that time. Alterations were made to the cathedral, covering it in stucco, by the first archbishop of Cartegena in the early 20th century.

Other beautiful churches include La Érmita (The Hermitage), a splendid gothic-style church located in Cali. The Carmelita Church in Medellín is another outstanding example of Spanish colonial church architecture.

The Cathedral of Zipa-quirá is located in a most unexpected place. Two hours north of Bogotá, the cathedral is built inside a huge salt mine!

LANGUAGE

SPANISH IS THE DOMINANT LANGUAGE in Colombia. It is also the official language. Colombians take pride in their style of language and are said to preserve the purest Spanish in Latin America.

Though there is remarkable ethnic diversity in the country, only about 4 percent of the population speak an indigenous Indian language. Of these, many speak Spanish as well. The inhabitants of the San Andrés and Providencia islands speak only English, which they inherited from the English Puritans who settled in these islands in the 17th century.

Regional accents differentiate the speech of Colombians living in different areas. The most distinguishable accent is heard on the Caribbean coast, where the spoken Spanish sounds more like that in the Dominican Republic or in Cuba than like that in Bogotá, Bucaramanga, or Medellín.

Left: **Most big cities in Colombia have public telephones in convenient locations.**

Opposite: **Colombians frequent bookstores and book fairs. Bogotá hosts an annual international book fair from late April to early May.**

THE SPANISH ALPHABET

The Spanish alphabet looks similar to the English alphabet, but it consists of 27 letters:

a, b, c, d, e, f, g, h, i, j, k, l, m, n, ñ, o, p, q, r, s, t, u, v, w, x, y, z

The letters *k* and *w* are generally found only in foreign words that have become part of the Spanish vocabulary. The *k* sound is represented in Spanish by *c* before *a*, *o*, and *u* and by *qu* before *e* and *i*.

Before 1994, the Spanish alphabet included the letters *ch* and *ll*. However, Spanish language academies around the world decided to drop *ch* and *ll* as separate letters when alphabetizing. While old Spanish dictionaries listed words beginning with *ch* after words beginning with *c*, most Spanish dictionaries now list words in the same order followed by English dictionaries. Thus, words beginning with *ch* are no longer listed in a separate section, but are treated as words beginning with *c*.

Spanish vowels often have accents, but these accented vowels are not considered separate letters, unlike in some other languages. Also, unlike in English, each Spanish vowel has one fundamental sound:

a   as in "m<u>a</u>ma"

e   as in "ch<u>e</u>ck"

i   as in "pol<u>i</u>ce"

o   as in "<u>o</u>r"

u   as in "r<u>u</u>de"

Many of the consonants have the same approximate sound as in English, though a linguist would consider these differences significant. Very noticeable distinctions are:

b and **v** are pronounced identically, as a "b."

d, when it is within a word, is pronounced like the English **th** in "then."

s is pronounced like the **s** in the English word "son."

ll, which represents one sound, is a blend of **l** and **y**, as in "ca<u>ll y</u>ou," or is often simply pronounced like **y**, as in "yore."

h is not pronounced in Spanish.

j has no exact English equivalent; a throaty **h** sound is the closest English comparison; this would also be the sound for **g** before **e** and **i**.

r, within a word, is a flapped sound like the **tt** in "kitty."

rr within a word is similar to the **r** sound described above; however it is trilled. (Note that *rr* is not officially a letter of the alphabet.)

NONVERBAL COMMUNICATION

There are not many differences between the gestures and nonverbal behavior of Colombians and North Americans, but there are a few worth mentioning.

Colombians gesture for people to come toward them in a manner similar to the North American wave, with the palm facing out. They indicate height in two ways. When describing an animal, they hold the hand as though it were resting on the animal's head. When describing a person, they hold the hand as though it were behind rather than above the person's head.

Etiquette is important. "Body language" taboos include entertaining a visitor barefoot, putting one's feet up on a desk or chair, slouching in a chair, yawning in public, and eating on the street.

Generally, Colombians living away from the coast are quite formal. They tend to express themselves verbally more than through movement and gestures. In Bogotá, for instance, the locals rarely use excited gestures or raise their voices when conveying their feelings or ideas. Their formality often keeps them from explicitly expressing their anger.

Instead, pretending not to hear or giving a slow response to an unwelcome question would be typical ways for inland Colombians to express their anger. Because of their formality, foreigners often perceive Colombians—especially those in Bogotá—as distant or cold. Residents of the coastal areas, however, tend to be more expressive nonverbally.

Colombians hold their hand palm outward as though it were behind the head when demonstrating a child's height.

GREETINGS

Greetings are an important part of Colombian etiquette. A verbal greeting is almost always accompanied by at least a handshake. Men shake hands with both women and men. Women sometimes shake hands with other women, frequently while grasping each other's right forearm. Close female friends often kiss one another on the cheek. Relatives or close male friends may hug.

Once first contact is accomplished, the greeting ritual continues with polite questioning about the well-being of each other's family members. Only then, after some small talk, is it appropriate to discuss business.

It is customary to have a short polite conversation before talking about business. To plunge straight into a business discussion would indicate a lack of social graces.

There are also procedures to follow when entering a group. Everyone must be greeted, at the very least with eye and verbal contact, and preferably with a handshake. It is also essential to say goodbye to everyone when leaving the group.

FORMS OF ADDRESS

When addressing someone, Colombians can use the familiar *tú* ("too") or the formal *usted* ("oos-TED"), both meaning "you." There are no exact guidelines. Among social equals, *usted* is used, but it changes to *tú* as the people get to know one another better. Persons of higher social status or those who are older may ask others to address them using *tú*, but Colombians may feel uncomfortable using the intimate form of address with persons of higher status. It is clearly not a simple matter!

Use of first names is equated with using *tú*, that is, with intimacy. So before acquaintances have reached a certain familiarity, they address one another as Señor and Señora.

NEWSPAPERS

Colombia has a free press, and the leading newspapers contain a wide range of international and national news, criticism, and commentary, plus special features.

Newspapers have always been the major source for an accurate picture of the general state of Colombia and a vehicle for political debate. The press has been a part of Colombian culture since 1791, when the first colonial newspaper, *Papel Periódico de la Ciudad de Santa Fe de Bogotá,* was founded.

There is a close relation between the government and the press, even though Colombian journalists generally maintain a strong belief in press freedom. For example, the two leading newspapers in Bogotá, *El Tiempo* and *El Espectador,* are identified with the Liberals, and two others, *La República* and *El Siglo,* support the Conservative Party. The most influential conservative paper in the country is *El Colombiano,* which is published in Medellín.

Colombia has a long press history. Newsstands carry local as well as international papers and magazines.

Colombians have a strong bias toward the truthfulness of the printed word; television and radio have been regulated by the government throughout the years. As a result, in this class-conscious nation, literacy has held a certain prestige that can be appreciated in this Colombian joke: "The country has two kinds of people, those with 'culture' and those with transistor radios."

Those interested in a more international news perspective can buy the *Miami Herald* in and around Bogotá and *The New York Times* and *The Wall Street Journal* at bookstores and newsstands in major cities.

ARTS

COLOMBIANS TAKE GREAT PRIDE in their artistic and cultural achievements. In fact, Bogotá has been called the "Athens of Latin America," in reference to the residents' appreciation and patronage of the arts. It is said with great pride that there are more bookstores lining the streets of the capital city than restaurants or cafés, and that more poets have become presidents than have generals.

The regionalism caused by Colombia's extreme geographical contrasts has also had an impact on the country's cultural and artistic life. Bogotá is best known for its literature and poetry, the Caribbean coast is famed for its songs and dances, and the people of Cali and Medellín focus their creative energies in industrial ventures. The religious festivals and rituals of the Roman Catholic Church are perhaps the only areas of creative expression shared by all Colombia's departments, or states.

Left: **Pottery is an ancient craft practiced today with little change in technique.**

Opposite: **A popular art market in Cali.**

87

Cuna Indians make a
necklace out of monkeys'
teeth. Local appreciation
of indigenous arts deve-
loped only in the 20th
century.

HISTORICAL BACKGROUND

Colombia's artistic and literary achievements fall into three periods: pre-Hispanic, colonial (when Colombia was a Spanish colony), and republican (after independence from Spain). While there was an obvious and marked transition from the first to the second era, the change from the colonial period to the republican period was much more gradual.

When the *conquistadores* arrived in Colombia, they destroyed any traditional Indian arts they encountered and insisted that all Colombian artistic expression be similar to styles and genres then popular in Spain. Their dislike for Indian art was evident in paintings and religious sculpture of the colonial period, although some churches built during that time housed indigenous Indian carvings. Most artistic works of the period were reminiscent of the Spanish style.

As the desire for independence grew, the Creoles (people of Spanish descent born in the New World) rejected everything that connected them with Spain, including artistic motifs. However, much of their inspiration was based on the contemporary artistic modes of other European countries, especially France.

It was only at the beginning of the 20th century that Colombians began to truly appreciate their indigenous artistic heritage, and what had been their mere acknowledgment of Indian monuments and colonial paintings grew into a great source of pride in their heritage and a basis for the creation of modern Colombian art forms.

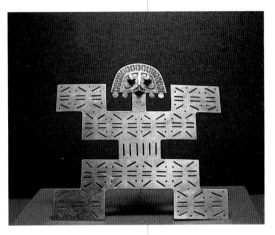

Beautiful gold treasures crafted by ancient Indians reveal a great mastery of metalwork techniques.

CHRONICLING THE TIMES

Gonzalo Jiménez de Quesada (1499–1579), the Spanish *conquistador* who founded Santa Fé de Bogotá—what is now Bogotá—in 1538, was also a prolific writer. He wrote several chronicles, pieces of descriptive and historical writing that *conquistadores* and men of letters sent back to Spain in order to inform the Spanish Crown of their discoveries.

A couple of decades after Jiménez de Quesada's death, Juan Rodríguez Freyle (1566–1640), who fought the Indians for many years before settling down near Bogotá, wrote the first widely-read chronicle of the conquest and settlement of Nueva Granada, which he called *El Carnero* (The Ram).

The monument of "The Old Shoes" stands by the roadside in Cartagena in memory of local poet Luis Carlos López.

LITERATURE

The most valuable Spanish contribution to the Colombian arts scene was in language and literature, dating back to Gonzalo Jiménez de Quesada, a lawyer-scholar-explorer. Colombia's first pieces of national literature came from the historical and descriptive writings of this *conquistador*.

Other leaders, such as Simón Bolívar, Camilo Torres, Antonio Nariño, and Francisco de Paula Santander, were both gifted writers and students of philosophy and European and American history. The 17th century was considered the baroque period in Latin American literature. The writing was exaggerated, flowery, and not particularly notable. The following century did not produce celebrated works either, which was perhaps a reflection of the decline of Spanish literature generally.

The 19th century, however, marked the beginning of significant Colombian literary output. *Tertulias* ("tayr-too-LEE-ahs"), or literary salons, began appearing, where patriots discussed forbidden books smuggled into the colony. This was the Romantic period in Colombian and world literature, and poetry was the major literary form. The works dealt with love, patriotism, nature, and religion. A leading Colombian religious poet of this time was José Eusebio Caro (1817–1853). Character development and a variety of metrical forms marked his works. So much creative energy went into poetry in the 19th century that few outstanding novels emerged.

In 1867, Jorge Isaacs wrote *Maria*, considered by many to be the first Latin American novel. At the end of the 19th century, Colombian poets and authors took part in a new literary movement called *modernismo* ("mo-der-NEES-mo"), Latin America's first original contribution to world literature. Famous literary figures from the modernist movement were José Asunción Silva (1865–96) and Guillermo Valencia (1873–1943).

Twentieth-century literature focused on realistic social commentary in the form of regional novels. Tomás Carrasquilla (1858–1940) wrote a novel about the mountain people of Antioquia; José Eustasio Rivera (1889–1928) dealt with Amazonian life in *La Vorágine* (*The Vortex*).

The 1960s brought a new literary age led by Gabriel García Márquez (b. 1928). His 1967 novel, *Cien Anos de Soledad* (*One Hundred Years of Solitude*), is one of the most widely read novels in the Spanish language since World War II. Many novelists have imitated his style, emphasizing social problems and the government's inability to solve them.

García Márquez received the 1982 Nobel prize for literature for his novels and short stories, which have been translated into many of the world's languages.

"Márquez has insights and sympathies which he can project with the intensity of a reflecting mirror in a bright sun."

— *New Statesman*

ART

Colombian visual art borrowed Spanish techniques and themes and received little attention until the 19th century, when the *costumbrista* ("cos-toom-BRIS-tah") movement began. This genre was concerned with the portrayal of customs, manners, and lifestyles.

The best known artist of the *costumbrista* era was Rámon Torres Méndez (1809–1885), whose series of paintings entitled *Cuadros de Costumbres* (*Pictures of Customs*) was an almost complete visual guide to life at the end of the 19th century.

The *costumbrista* period was followed by one of great interest in realism and impressionism, inspired by the French movement.

At Cali's Cañas Gordas Hacienda, an art class becomes an enjoyable outdoor experience.

ART THAT REACHES OUT TO PEOPLE

Roldanillo, a rural town of 50,000 inhabitants, is more than 400 years old. Throughout its lengthy history, most of its sons have lived by farming and cattle raising—except Omar Rayo (b. 1928), an artist of world renown and the force behind Roldanillo's imaginative Rayo Museum for Latin American Prints and Drawings.

Nearly hidden in the center of the peaceful and traditional town, the museum is a strikingly beautiful collection of eight one-room spaces that are naturally lit by glass-domed ceilings. The museum is devoted to works on paper and is the only one of its kind in Latin America.

Rayo has been living in New York in self-exile since 1960, but his commitment to his birthplace has inspired him to return and share his art. The museum is not, however, merely an exhibition of his works. It is a workshop-museum where lithography, photography, and photoengraving are also taught. Other artists exhibit at the Rayo Museum as well as teach and create new pieces.

In conjunction with the museum, there is also an exhibit on the highway leading from Cali to Roldanillo that displays on billboards works by 19 artists, including Fernando Botero and Mario Toral. The highway museum, called Arte Vial, brings art out into the street to be viewed by all, even those who do not visit museums. It is the hope of Omar Rayo that young people in rural areas will now have the opportunity to become increasingly aware of the beauty of modern art through Arte Vial and the Rayo Museum.

Artists in the 20th century introduced progressive works following international trends. Alejandro Obregón (b. 1920) is considered by some critics to be the best Colombian artist alive. Fernando Botero (b. 1932) is another world-renowned artist.

Other distinguished artists in Colombia include Judith Márquez Montoya, who has gained recognition with her many series of canvases on similar themes, and Ana Mercedes Hoyos (b. 1942), who has experimented with a "pop" style, with surrealism, and with exacting treatments of everyday objects.

ARCHITECTURE

Colombia's colonial architecture was consistent with Spanish styles and varied according to the climate in which it was being developed and according to the province from which the colonists originated. Fine colonial architecture can be seen in Santa Marta, Cartagena, Bogotá, Tunja, and Popayán.

Ultramodern buildings are being constructed in the cities. In Bogotá, wide boulevards with tall glass skyscrapers create a magnificent contrast to the impressive colonial quarter. Many modern Colombian architects have studied with leading architects in Europe and the United States, and architecture has become a very prestigious field. Works of particular merit include the Bank of Bogotá, Cartagena's baseball stadium, and the Ángel Arango Library.

Modern architecture is consistent with Medellín's evolution as a center of technology.

Musicians give a lively performance at a music festival.

PERFORMING AND FOLK ARTS

Afro-Colombians and indigenous Indians have had a strong influence on music in the coastal regions. Afro-Colombian rhythms such as *fandangos* ("fan-DAHN-gos"), *porros* ("POR-ros"), and *mapales* ("MAH-plays") have also gained attention outside the country.

DANCE Folk dance ranges from the coast's exciting rhythmic steps to the *bambuco* ("bam-BOO-ko"), which resembles a waltz at a slightly quicker tempo. The *bambuco* is the national dance and is performed by couples. The *salsa* ("SAHL-sa") is a lively dance in which everyone whirls to trumpets and *maracas* ("mar-RAH-cas"). The *cumbia* ("COOM-bee-ah") is an African-Colombian rhythm that has its listeners tapping their feet.

MUSIC Instruments typically used in Colombian music are the *flauta* ("FLAO-tah"), which is an Indian flute, the *tiple* ("TEE-play"), which is a many-stringed guitar-like instrument, and the *raspa* ("RAHS-pah"), which is made from a gourd and played like a washboard.

In the Popayán region, two types of traditional music prevail: the *murga* ("MOOR-gah") and the *chirimia* ("che-re-MEE-ah"). The *murga* is performed by wandering bands of musicians playing *tiples* ("TEE-plays"), *bandolas* ("ban-DOH-las"), guitars, mandolins, and accordions. *Chirimia* music is characteristic of the music of the indigenous Indians of the lower

The *cumbia* is a lively dance accompanied by African-Colombian music.

Andes. Though folk music is the dominant type of music, Colombians do also enjoy classical music. Bogotá is home to the National Symphony Orchestra and the National Conservatory founded in 1882. Concerts and operas are held in Bogotá's Colon Theater.

DRAMA Colombia has a long-standing dramatic tradition. The country's first theater was established in the late 1700s. José Fernández Madrid (1789–1830) was considered the founder of the national theater, because he was the first Colombian dramatist to write about the New World.

Today, Colombian drama is thriving, not just in the numerous theaters around the country, but also on the silver screen. *Rodrigo D: No Future* (1990), directed by Victor Gaviria in a quasi-documentary style, was the first Colombian film to be showcased in the Cannes Film Festival.

LEISURE

COLOMBIA'S VARIED LANDSCAPE permits a great variety of outdoor activities. As in most Latin American countries, soccer is by far the favorite sport, though baseball and basketball have their share of devotees. The women's basketball league consists of teams representing the departments, or states, of the country. Colombian players also regularly participate in international table tennis competitions.

There is much greater access to recreational facilities in the cities than in rural areas. In Bogotá, for example, there are countless opportunities for spectator and competitor alike, such as boxing tournaments in the Coliseo El Salitre and auto racing events. Golf, tennis, bowling, and skiing are also popular, but are generally affordable only to the very wealthy.

Left: **In Cartagena, a leisurely day at the Bocagrande Beach is enjoyed by many.**

Opposite: **Like soccer, cycling is a popular sport in Colombia. Cycling races attract many participants and spectators.**

WATER SPORTS

Water sports are quite popular among Colombians. They enjoy fishing for marlin, tarpon, dolphin, tuna, and sailfish any time of the year, and international fishing competitions are held in Barranquilla in the months of May and November.

The coast offers great opportunities for surfers. Swimming, water skiing, scuba-diving, and snorkelling are exciting diversions in the inlets and bays of the Pacific. The Rosario Islands off Cartagena are a favorite place for skin-diving, but only for the very daring—sharks and barracuda frequent these tempting, clear waters.

Skiing is an exhilarating experience on the slopes of the Nevado del Ruiz.

MOUNTAINEERING

Scaling Colombia's mountains is a popular pastime, as are cycling and hiking. The Sierra Nevada, approximately 30 miles (48 km) from Santa Marta, provides one of the most exciting mountain climbing experiences to be had anywhere in the world. The peaks of the Sierra Nevada are nearly 19,000 feet (5,791 m) high.

HUNTING

Game hunting has long been a favored sport among the wealthy. With tapirs, deer, and boar roaming the wilderness and organized safaris in the *llanos* of the Amazon basin, game hunters are never bored. Serious dove hunters have been visiting the Cauca Valley near Cali since 1975.

City dwellers are aware that sports and regular exercise are good for the health and raise one's fitness level.

A bullfight pits the courage of the *matador* against the strength of the bull. This is why it is known as *la fiesta brava* (the brave festival).

BULLFIGHTS

Bullfights are so popular that there are two bullfighters' unions, and most cities have *plazas de toros* (PLAH-sahs deh TOH-ros"), bullfighting rings. There are bullfights all year round, but the most exciting ones are the international festivals in February and December, when visiting *toreros* ("to-RAY-ros"), or bullfighters, arrive. Though bullfighting is a dangerous profession, it is a matter of grace, courage, and skill for the *matador* ("mah-tah-DOR"), the bullfighter who kills the bull. The bulls are bred specifically for fighting. They are aggressive, obstinate, and extremely strong.

Bullfights take place on Thursday and Sunday afternoons. In a typical program, three *matadores* fight two bulls each. Before the contest, they parade around the arena in their beautifully hand-tailored suits, called *trajes de luces* ("TRAH-hay de LOO-ses"), suits of lights. The *matadores* head the procession, armed with swords and followed by six-man teams of *picadores* ("pee-cah-DOH-rehs") to assist them. The crowds are screaming at fever-pitch by the time the parade is over, and then the bullfight begins. A trumpet sounds, the bull pen opens, and the bull charges out into the ring.

The *picadores* begin to taunt the bull so that the *matador* can observe its movements. He performs a few moves with the cape, called passes, without moving his feet. Then the *picadores* harass the bull by prodding its shoulders with lances, weakening its neck muscles. The *banderilleros* ("ban-day-reel-LYAY-ros") insert darts into the bull's upper back. Attached to the darts are ribbons, which are included for color.

For the third and final act, the *matador* first prepares the bull for the kill by means of a few graceful maneuvers. Well-executed passes draw cheers of "*Olé!*" from the crowd. After what the *matador* feels is the correct number of passes, he goes for the kill with a single swift thrust of the sword.

Although bullfighting is a cruel sport condemned by animal rights supporters, it still draws excited crowds to bullrings in most Spanish-speaking countries.

The most admired method of killing the bull is called the *recibiendo* ("ray-see-be-EN-do"). It is a perfectly executed thrust between the horns that kills the bull instantly. This maneuver is quite dangerous, for the *matador* must stand perfectly still while the enraged animal lunges toward him.

The more common procedure is the *volapié* ("vo-LAH-pe-ay"), which allows the *matador* to dodge the charging bull and deliver the fatal blow between the shoulder blades. This is a dangerous sport, for a simple movement of the bull's horns can gore the *matador*. If the *matador* has performed successfully, the bull dies immediately and the crowd cheers.

COCKFIGHTS

Cockfights are popular among Colombians. Trained gamecocks are put beak to beak on a stage or in a pit and are let loose to fight one another. The game-cocks are usually fitted with razor-sharp spurs. The competition goes on until one of the cocks is either killed, can no longer fight, or refuses to fight.

There are three types of cockfights: the single battle, in which two cocks fight; the main battle, in which cocks are paired and play an elimination tournament; and the battle royal, in which several cocks fight one another until only one is left standing.

Cockfighting is one of the many games on which Colombians like to bet.

BETTING

An activity that is very popular among both rich and poor is gambling on games of chance. Estimates indicate that Colombians spend as much as 25 percent of their regular income on gambling, regardless of how small or large that income is.

Lotteries are prevalent throughout the country. They are thought to serve an important social function, because the country's welfare program and hospitals receive a generous portion of the profits.

In addition to this government-sponsored activity, there are numerous gambling casinos and horseracing tracks, and there is always considerable wagering on other sporting events, such as soccer, bullfights, and cockfights.

SPORTS IN RURAL AREAS

In rural areas, there are sports clubs and leagues affiliated with the local churches or sponsored by municipalities. Chess, bicycle races, soccer, volleyball, and *tejo* ("TAY-ho") are the activities most likely to occupy the residents of the countryside in their recreational time.

One of Colombia's traditional games is *tejo*, which generates a lot of noise and excitement.

TEJO

Tejo is a traditional game similar to horseshoes. Nearly every Colombian town has a *tejo* court. Two mounds of dirt are built around pipes that are set about 40 feet (12 m) apart. The tops of the pipes are level with the tops of the mounds of dirt and are loaded with small amounts of gunpowder, called *mecha* ("MAY-chah"). The *tejo*, a smooth round piece of metal or stone, is thrown at the top of the mound, and the object of the game is to explode the *mecha*.

There are *tejo* experts throughout the countryside, and on Sundays after church or in the afternoons on market days, the sound of exploding *mechas* provides much excitement and commotion.

105

FESTIVALS

THE WORD "FIESTA" brings to mind a whimsical celebration with laughter, dancing, music, and merriment. There may be much ringing of church bells and even fireworks. However, there is usually a serious reason behind the activities, and often a somber tone pervades the celebration of these special events.

Opposite: **Colombians put on special costumes at Carnival time.**

FIESTA Fiestas in Colombia are held to commemorate milestones in the life of the nation or of its communities. Fiestas of indigenous groups may mark the harvest, a child's first haircut, or seasonal changes, such as the beginning of the rainy season. Civic festivities usually include speeches, parades, and sometimes athletic competitions.

Religious fiestas are usually the most numerous and most colorful. While there is a serious and solemn background to each feast day, the purpose behind the celebration is both religious and entertaining. Generally, a rural fiesta will emphasize the worship aspect. Special Masses mark the day as well as a procession that features a holy image and great ceremony. Often a market day will be coordinated with the activities so vendors can display their wares for a large crowd.

Above: **In Cali, a caval-cade along the main streets of the town usually opens the annual fair.**

The allegorical float procession held on Epiphany in Tuquerres is a most colorful event.

FERIAS

Fiestas that are associated with a religious pilgrimage and that last a week or more are called *ferias* ("FAY-re-ahs"). Dancing is usually part of the religious fiesta. Two kinds of dance are usually performed at *ferias*: ritual and folk dances.

Ritual dances take place in the courtyard or main grounds of the church. Women generally do not take part in them. A ritual dance is considered a serious matter and usually includes a dramatization and dialogue for a specific purpose such as honoring a saint. Alternatively, a folk dance is a social matter. Its main purpose is to entertain, and it can be performed by men and women of all ages.

Some of the most colorful festivals are those of the indigenous groups and Caribbean Africans. Among the Andean groups, as a result of missionary efforts, there has been a blending of Christian saints and pagan gods. For example, many indigenous Indians do not see much difference between the Mama (Mother Nature) and the Virgin Mary. Coastal Africans have combined their traditional rituals and beliefs with those of Christianity.

Regardless of whether the celebration is strictly Christian, an Indian ritual, or a hodgepodge of African, Christian, and pagan ceremonies, the fiesta is an opportunity to bring zest and color into lives that are often a simple and trying struggle. The fiesta is a wonderful contrast to the everyday routine of labor and poverty. Because it occurs yearly, it is a magical time for all to anticipate. It becomes a project for all in the community to plan and revel in when spirited times begin.

The festival of Colombia's national patron, the Virgin Mary of the Rosary of Chinquinquirá, is one of the most famous in the Americas.

SAN ISIDRO

April marks the end of the dry season. On April 4, the image of San Isidro (St. Isadore the Farmer), who is responsible for bringing the rains, is carried through the town of Río Frío. All the townspeople follow his image and chant his praises.

In their chanting, the local farmers explain the need for rain, and optimally, San Isidro will cooperate by bringing the first shower before the celebration is completed. So as not to demand too much of the saint, the parade is slow and drawn out. For every two steps participants take, they take one step back!

If San Isidro has not cooperated after several processions through the town, the tone of the chanting changes from praise to scolding. As the hours pass, the yelling becomes progressively more belligerent until the townspeople can be heard screaming profanities! Should there be no change in the skies, San Isidro is put away until the next April, when the worshipers will hope for better results.

DÍA DE NEGRITOS/FIESTA DE LOS BLANQUITOS

Chirimias, groups of strolling musicians, take to the streets to create an air of fanfare during the carnivals of the blacks and the whites.

In Popayán, during the first week of January, there is a Mardi Gras atmosphere to celebrate the end of the Christmas season. January 5 is the Día de Negritos (Day of the Black Ones), and the next day is the Fiesta de los Blanquitos (Festival of the White Ones). Many people think that the color references are to the biblical Three Wise Men, who reached their destination on the sixth day of the month. However, the days actually get their names from the activities that take place then.

On the morning of the Día de Negritos, boys with shoe polish chase the girls of the community and decorate them with their blackened hands. As the day progresses, older boys chase after older girls, and by the time evening falls, no one is safe from the marauding boys.

The frivolity of present-day celebrations of the Día de Negritos derives from more dignified practices in days of old, when gentlemen would parade beneath balconies until the ladies came to the door. The men were then allowed to paint a spot on the ladies' cheek or forehead. The festivities have grown more rowdy over the years, and today many people prefer to stay indoors to avoid the fracas.

There are still street parades in the afternoon with people in masquerade

and *chirimias*, or strolling groups, playing the latest Colombian *bambucos* on traditional instruments. At the main square, the *tasajo* ("tay-SAH-ho"), or distribution of foods donated by rich farmowners, takes place. When night falls, the celebrations continue at a social club or in private homes, with dancing and partying until dawn.

The following morning, white becomes the focus of the celebration. Boys chase girls in the streets with white flour and ride around town tossing the flour on everyone they see. People on balconies pour water on the flour-coated pedestrians, until everyone is laden with a sticky mixture. There is much merrymaking and drinking. Older Colombians may recall how the day was once marked by beautiful religious celebrations.

Masquerades add to the Mardi Gras atmosphere during the Fiesta de los Blanquitos.

The word "carnival" evokes a vision of glittering costumes and unending merrymaking, but Colombian carnivals are more subdued than those in other parts of South America. Still, there is much dancing in the street.

Music, on its own or as accompaniment, is an important element of carnivals all over the world.

CARNIVAL

The word "carnival" comes from the Latin *carne vale* (farewell to flesh), which aptly describes the fasting of Lent in the days leading up to Easter. The philosophy behind the carousing is that indulgence in one's desires before the fast will make it easier to realize the oncoming religious experience. The whole country participates in the festivities of Carnival. However, the celebration in Barranquilla is most famous. The city begins preparing for Carnival just after Christmas, and the two months preceding Lent are filled with masquerades and dancing in the public square.

Several ritual dances are performed during Carnival: the *maestranza* is a comical dance performed by men dressed as women; the *danza de los pájaros* ("DAHN-sah de los pah-HOH-ros") is also danced by men wearing colorful costumes, including plumage and masks with beaks.

The *coyongo* ("co-YON-go") is a ritual dance-drama. A *coyongo* is a large aquatic fishing bird. In this dance, several "birdmen" circle a man dressed as a fish, who tries to evade the "birdmen," as they close in on him.

INDEPENDENCE OF CARTAGENA

This annual carnival takes place on the November 11 anniversary of the Declaration of Independence. The old walled city holds a four-day celebration featuring thousands of costumed people dancing in the streets to the sound of *maracas* and drums. There are parades, floral displays, and frenzied excitement caused by fireworks called *buscapiés* ("boos-cah-PYESS"), or feet searchers, that send crowds reeling as the firecrackers bounce along the streets.

People dance throughout the night and wander in the streets to the music of guitars, *maracas,* and drums. The festivities culminate with the National Beauty Contest's selection of the young woman who will represent Colombia in international beauty contests.

CALENDAR OF FESTIVALS

January	1	New Year's Day
	6	Epiphany Day
February	2	Candlemas
March	19	St. Joseph's Day
March/April		Maundy Thursday
		Good Friday
		Holy Saturday
		Easter
May	1	Labor Day
		Ascension Day
June		Corpus Christi
June	29	Sts. Peter and Paul Day
July	20	Independence Day
August	7	Battle of Boyacá
	15	Feast of the Assumption
October	12	Columbus Day
November	1	All Saints Day
	11	Independence of Cartagena
December	8	Feast of the Immaculate Conception
	25	Christmas

FOOD

COLOMBIAN FOOD generally uses a lot of potatoes and rice, and stews and soups also feature prominently on the Colombian menu. Poultry is the preferred meat. In recent years, meat consumption in the country has shifted away from beef, as poultry can be bought at lower prices and is considered a healthier meat alternative. Coffee is the national drink, found in almost every Colombian household. According to a survey conducted in 1999, nearly 90 percent of all households in Colombia served coffee at least once a day.

The Colombian kitchen is simply the room in which meals are prepared. The family does not eat in the kitchen; they eat in the dining room instead. Colombian homes do not have dine-in kitchens or breakfast nooks like those that are common in the United States. Nearly all rural homes in Colombia now have electrical power and a running water supply. However, rural kitchens may not be equipped with electrical appliances used in urban homes, such as microwave ovens.

Colombians have a strong cultural bias against standing water. As a result, they prefer not to leave dirty plates to soak in the sink. Instead they wash their dishes immediately under running water. Maids seldom close the drain in the sink or collect water in a dishpan to clean up after a meal. Rather, they keep the water running, scrape everything off the dish, and then wash it with a soapy sponge before rinsing it under the running faucet.

Preparing a meal in a spacious Colombian kitchen.

Hot water heaters are also not common in Colombia. In rural areas, water for cooking, bathing, and washing clothes is boiled in a large pot over the fire or gas stove. City dwellers have water heaters that must be lit. Because gas is costly, some families have the maid light the water heater each morning so that there is sufficient water for the family to shower, and it is routinely turned off after breakfast.

As a result, dishes are washed in cold water. It is customary to leave the water running for long periods of time. It also makes perfect sense not to soak the dishes, for dirty dishes bathed in cold water would certainly lead to an unsavory mess!

THE NATIONAL DRINK

There are four types of Colombian coffee: *caturra* ("kah-TOO-rah"), *maragojipe* ("mah-rah-goh-HEE-pay"), *pajarito* ("pah-hah-REE-to"), and *borbón* ("bor-BON"). Coffee plants are grown under banana trees, which shade them from direct sunlight. Because only the ripest beans can be harvested, they must be hand-picked and dried on racks for several days. In some villages, it is the job of the children to turn the beans so that both sides are thoroughly dried.

Supremo ("so-PRAY-mo") is the highest grade of bean; *extra* ("EX-trah") is a lower grade. *Excelso* ("ex-SAHL-so") is a blend of the high- and lower-grade beans. This blend of coffee is exported to the United States in larger quantities than any other coffee.

In Colombia, meals often come with a serving of coffee. A small cup of black coffee is called a *tinto*, and it often contains as much sugar as coffee. Coffee with milk is known as *café perico* ("kah-FAY pay-REE-co"); *café con leche* ("kah-FAY con LAY-chay") is warm milk with coffee.

There are no coffee breaks in Colombian offices, because people drink coffee round-the-clock. Instead, a woman travels from desk to desk and dispenses *tintos*. A typical Colombian between the ages of 12 and 64 consumes at lease one cup of coffee a day.

FOOD SHOPPING

Shopping in Colombia's major cities is very similar to shopping in the United States. Colombia has one of the most modern supermarket sectors in Latin America. The large supermarket chains are Cafam, Carulla, Fortuna, Ley, and Olímpica, and there are also hypermarkets, such as Carrefour. Almost any item can be found in the city, but many foods are imported and are only available in delicatessens and speciality stores.

A wide variety of fruits and vegetables is available throughout the year. They are usually moderately priced, but fruits imported from the United States, such as pears, apples, and plums, can be costly. Meats are a bit less expensive than in the United States. Yet they are usually leaner—because the animals are grass-fed—and taste somewhat different—because they are fresh. In small towns or in the neighborhood meat market, there may be no refrigeration. When pork or beef arrives from the slaughterhouse, a red flag is hung out so that customers know the meat has arrived. They buy up the meat quickly and take it home to prepare the next meal.

Rural villages usually have a small store, or *tienda* ("tee-AYN-dah"), where people buy cigarettes, food, beer, and other items. The *tienda* is also a social center, where villagers come to visit and share gossip. A *tienda* may be no more than a room, perhaps attached to the owner's house, with a counter where employees gather merchandise for customers.

Most Colombian towns and villages have more than one *tienda*, and these *tiendas* open all day. The *tienda* competes with the modern convenience store and the large supermarket by offering its wide middle- and lower-income consumer base advantages such as proximity and credit.

121

On market days, food stalls sell a variety of local dishes. Notice that the left hand is always above the table.

MEALTIMES

Breakfast, lunch, and dinner are traditional mealtimes in Colombia. Breakfast is not a family meal, and everyone eats according to the needs of his or her personal schedule. The father, who may have to leave for work as early as 7 A.M., will eat breakfast earliest. The children's breakfast time depends on whether they have to go to school and what time the school bus picks them up. Breakfast foods vary by region, but usually include eggs, soup, bread, fruit, juice, and of course coffee.

Lunch, on the other hand, is the most important meal for the family, and the father returns home for it. This may be his only opportunity to spend time with his children, since he may not return home in the evening before their bedtime. Lunch is eaten at around 12:30 or 1 P.M. and may last till 2:30 P.M. Soup, rice, meat with vegetables, and dessert are the typical courses for the midday meal.

The evening meal, eaten at around 7 or 8 P.M., may include soup, rice, meat, potatoes, salad, and beans.

TABLE MANNERS

Table manners in the Colombian home are similar to those in homes in the United States. One practice that is different, however, is that Colombians feel that the left hand should be kept visible above the table.

Colombians are quite formal at mealtimes. Wearing pajamas or a bathrobe and slippers to breakfast is not acceptable. At lunch and dinner, everyone in the family is expected to dress as though they were ready to dine out. Pleasant conversation is always welcome during meals, and it is considered impolite to eat too much or to take food without first offering it to others. If the host offers more refreshments, the guest politely decines. When a person has finished eating, he or she places the silverware horizontally across the plate.

HIGH ALTITUDE COOKING

In Medellín, Bogotá, and other regions above 5,000 feet (1,524 m), people practice high-altitude cooking. Because air has less pressure at higher altitudes, recipes must be modified if the quality of the food being cooked is to be preserved.

Foods that suffer most from changes in altitude are those that require baking or boiling and those that contain a lot of sugar. Water boils at a higher temperature at higher altitudes, so it takes longer to prepare boiled foods. Pressure cookers are quite helpful in such cases.

Since most breads and cakes depend on yeast or baking powder for their shape and consistency, the decreased pressure makes it necessary to reduce the leavening agents so cakes and breads do not collapse. For baking in the highlands, the rule-of-thumb is to reduce baking powder, shortening, and sugar slightly and increase eggs and liquid slightly.

FOODS OF COLOMBIA

Colombian foods are rich and heavily seasoned, but not necessarily spicy. Starches are a large part of the Colombian diet, including potatoes, rice, and a root called *yuca* ("YOO-kah"). Generally, the Colombian menu is a mixture of Indian and Spanish traditions. What individuals select from a menu reflects economic status and regional tastes.

A dish that is popular throughout the country is *ajiaco* ("ah-hee-AH-coh"), a highly seasoned soup of potatoes, chicken, capers, corn, and slices of avocado. Soup is served much more often and in many more varieties in Colombia than in the United States. It is even occasionally served as breakfast or as a main course. *Changua* ("chan-GOO-ah") soup is a favorite Andean breakfast. It is a blend of beef broth, milk, and chopped coriander.

Sopa de pan ("SO-pah de pahn") is a main course soup that uses bread, eggs, and cheese. It is quite filling and full of nutrients. Other popular soups are made with vegetable, plantain (a fruit similar to banana), rice, and potato.

Some very tasty breads are served in Colombia. *Arepa* ("ah-RAY-pah") is a simple cornbread of Indian origin. It is made of ground corn mixed with a little salt and enough water to make a stiff dough, which

Beef is the most plentiful meat in Colombia, and in rural areas, it is broiled over a charcoal fire by the roadside.

is then toasted on a greased griddle. *Arepas* are eaten by rich and poor alike. *Mogollos* ("mo-GOL-lyos") are whole wheat muffins with a raisin-flavored center that are served with dinner. *Roscones* ("ros-KO-nes") are buns filled with guava jelly and sprinkled with sugar.

Colombian beef is somewhat tougher than beef from the United States, but Colombian cooks have found some wonderfully tasty ways to tenderize and prepare it. Rather than grinding the beef into hamburger meat, they slice it into tiny cubes. The meat is sautéed, broiled, or added to soups. The small size of the cubes prevents the meat from becoming tough. Another zesty Colombian tenderizing method is to simmer a chunk of meat for several hours and then baste and roast it for several more.

The *arepa* is a tasty cornbread enjoyed by all Colombians.

REGIONAL DELICACIES

Regional favorites have much to do with what types of vegetables and fruits grow in the area. For example, the high, cool mountain valleys near Bogotá produce white potatoes in abundance, and recipes of that region make good use of this vegetable. *Papas chorreadas* ("PAH-pas chor-ray-AH-das") are boiled potatoes covered with a flavorful sauce of coriander, cream, tomatoes, cheese, and scallions.

Though the region around Bogotá is cool, the warm zones are quite close by, and the cooks of the capital city have an abundance of tropical fruits available to them. Bananas and avocados are favored ingredients. There are perhaps a dozen ways that the people of Bogotá prepare green bananas. Avocados are added to all types of salads and soups.

People of Indian and African descent who inhabit the jungles grow *yuca*, corn, beans, and plantains, and they catch local wildlife for meat. They eat monkeys, tapirs, and any kind of bird, except parrot, whose flesh is too tough. Ants are a delicacy among Colombian villagers and jungle dwellers. The insects are caught in large quantities during mating season and are fried in oil or fat.

In the western part of the country, particularly the Cauca valley, there is a distinctive local cuisine that makes wonderful use of *yuca* and plantain that thrive in the warm climate. The leathery leaves of the plantain are used to wrap various mixtures of corn and other ingredients for steaming and boiling. One such treat is *hallaca* ("hay-YAH-kah"), which is similar to the *tamales* ("tah-MAHL-les") of Mexico.

The Colombian *hallaca* makes use of plantain leaves to wrap the ingredients instead of the cornhusk favored in Mexico.

PAPAS CHORREADAS

2 tablespoons butter
4 scallions
½ cup finely chopped onions
5 tomatoes, peeled, seeded
 and chopped
½ cup heavy cream

1 teaspoon coriander
¼ teaspoon dried oregano
pinch of cumin
½ teaspoon salt
1 cup grated mozzarella cheese
8 large potatoes, peeled and boiled

1. Heat butter over moderate heat in a 10-inch (25.4-cm) skillet.
2. Add scallions and onions and stir frequently for five minutes or until onions are soft and transparent.
3. Add tomatoes and cook, stirring for five minutes.
4. Add cream, coriander, oregano, cumin, and salt, stirring constantly.
5. Continue stirring and add cheese. Stir until cheese melts.
6. Serve over sliced boiled potatoes.

Restaurants in rural areas may be no more than boards held by wooden poles, where local people come for a drink and a bite to eat.

DINING OUT

There is an exciting variety of international restaurants in the larger cities, especially in Bogotá, where there are restaurants serving Swiss, Middle Eastern, and other cuisines.

However, many Colombian restaurants take pride in serving dishes typical of their region. At finer restaurants, waiters are particularly polite and provide excellent service. There may be as many as three to four waiters per table to serve the diners' every need.

Fast food lovers can find some of their favorites in Bogotá. Burger King and Pizza Hut outlets dot the city streets. There are also local hamburger shops in all the major cities, and *cantinas* ("kan-TEE-nahs") sell snacks, tropical fruit juices, and coffee. Bogotá also has many bars, cafés, and nightclubs for after-dinner entertainment.

DRINKING CUSTOMS

Colombians do not drink much at meals. Coffee, however, being the national beverage, is often consumed with meals. Children usually take milk with their meals. Fruit juices and colas are favorite soft drinks, and they are usually highly sweetened, since Colombians love sugar.

The hosts of a party always encourage their guests to have an alcohol beverage, and declining an invitation to "join the party" would be regarded as snobbish behavior.

Beer is a favorite drink between meals, and in rural areas, it is occasionally taken with meals. Wine is served at dinner, when there are guests, but it is not typically served at family meals. Colombia produces very little wine, and imported wines can be very expensive.

A traditional Indian alcoholic beverage is a potent corn liquor called *chica* ("CHEE-kah"). Though the government outlawed *chica* in 1948, the drink's popularity has not suffered, especially in the rural areas, where alcohol is an important part of community life on market days, on visits to the *tienda*, and on other occasions.

Cuna Indians prepare their own drink with bananas.

Other favorite Colombian liquors are rum, a fermented brown sugar called *guarapo* ("gwa-RAH-po"), and a licorice-flavored liquor called *aguardiente* ("ah-goo-ahr-dee-AYN-tay"). Every department produces its own brand of *aguardiente*, a great source of pride for the residents.

AJIACO DE POLLO BOGOTANO (BOGOTA CHICKEN SOUP)

This recipe serves six people.

2 ounces (56.7 g) butter
3 pounds (1.4 kg) chicken serving pieces
2 finely chopped large onions
8 thinly sliced medium potatoes
3 pints (1.4 l) chicken stock
6 new, or small red, potatoes

2 ears of corn, each cut into 3 pieces
3 tablespoons (44.4 ml) capers
1 pint (0.5 l) double cream
Salt and pepper
Cumin seeds (optional)

Heat butter in a heavy casserole dish, and sauté chicken pieces with onion until chicken is golden. Add thinly sliced potatoes and chicken stock. Cover and cook over low heat for about 25 minutes. Add new potatoes and cook for about 20 minutes or until chicken and new potatoes are tender. Remove chicken pieces and new potatoes, and work stock through a sieve. Return stock to the casserole, and season with cumin, salt, and pepper to taste. Add chicken and potatoes, corn, and capers. Simmer for 5 minutes. Add cream and simmer just long enough to heat through. Serve in deep soup plates.

EMPANADAS

This recipe makes six servings.

$^1/_4$ cup (59 ml) raisins
1 tablespoon (14.8 ml) apple cider vinegar
1 pound (0.5 kg) ground beef or turkey
1 small chopped onion
2 cloves finely chopped garlic
$1^3/_4$ cups (414 ml) salsa
$^1/_4$ cup (59 ml) slivered almonds

2 tablespoons (29.6 ml) brown sugar
$^1/_2$ teaspoon (2.5 ml) ground cinnamon
$^1/_4$ teaspoon (1.2 ml) salt
$^1/_2$ cup (118 ml) shredded cheddar cheese
1 pound (0.5 kg) frozen bread dough, thawed
1 lightly beaten egg

Preheat oven to 375°F (191°C). Combine raisins and vinegar in small bowl. Soak for 15 to 20 minutes or until raisins are plump. Cook meat (beef or turkey), onion, and garlic in a large skillet until meat is browned. Drain. Add $^1/_2$ cup (118 ml) salsa, almonds, raisins, sugar, cinnamon, and salt. Bring to a boil. Cook for 3 to 4 minutes or until flavors are blended. Divide dough into 6 pieces and roll into balls. On a well-floured board, roll each ball into a 6-inch (15.2-cm) circle. Place $^1/_2$ cup (118 ml) meat filling on bottom half of circle. Sprinkle with cheese. Fold top half of dough over filling. Crimp edges with tines of a fork. Pierce top with the fork. Place on a greased cookie sheet. Brush with egg. Bake for 20 to 25 minutes or until golden. Serve with remaining salsa.

MAP OF COLOMBIA

Amazonas state, B4, B5, C4, C5, D4, D5

Amazon River, C5, D5

Antioquia state, A2, B2, B3

Arauca state, C2, D2

Atlántico state, B1

Atrato River, A2, B2, B3

Barranquilla, B1

Bogotá, B3

Bolívar state, B1, B2

Boyacá, B2, B3, C2, C3

Brazil, C4, C5, D4, D5

Bucaramanga, C2

Buenos Aires, B4

Caldas state, B3

Cali, B3

Caquetá River, B4, C4, C5, D5

Caquetá state, B3, B4, C4

Caribbean Sea, A1, A2, B1, B2

Cartagena, B1

Casanare, C2, C3

Cauca River, B2, B3

Cauca state, A3, A4, B3, B4

César River, B1, B2

César state, B1, B2, C1, C2

Chocó state, A2, A3, B2, B3

Cordillera Central, B2, B3

Cordillera Occidental, A3, A4, B2, B3

Cordillera Oriental, B3, B4, C2, C3

Córdoba, B1, B2

Cúcuta, C2

Cundinamarca, B3

Ecuador, A4, A5, B4, B5

Equator, A4–D4

Guainía state, C3, C4, D3, D4

Guajira Peninsula, C1

Guaviare River, B4, C3, D3

Guaviare State, B4, C3, C4

Huila state, B3, B4

Ibagué, B3

Isla Fuerte, B1

Islas del Rosario, B1

La Guajira state, C1

Llanos, C2, C3

Magdalena River, B1, B2

Magdalena state, B1, B2

Manizales, B3

Medellín, B2

Meta River, C2

Meta state, B3, B4, C3

Montería, B2

Nariño state, A3, A4

Norte de Santander state, B2, C2

Orinoco river, D2, D3

Pacific Ocean, A2–A4

Panama, A1, A2

Pereira, B3

Peru, A5, B4, B5, C5

Popayán, B3

Putumayo River, C5, D5

Putumayo state, A4, B4

Quindío state, B3

Risaralda state, B2, B3

San Andrés y Providencia, A1

Santa Marta, B1

Santander state, B2, B3, C2, C3

Sinú River, B1, B2

Sucre state, B1, B2

Tumaco, A4

Tunja, B3

Valle state, A3, B3

Vaupés River, C4

Vaupés state, C4

Venezuela, C1, C2, D1, D2

Villavicencio, B3

ECONOMIC COLOMBIA

Natural Resources

Coal

Fishing

Gems

Gold

Hydroelectricity

Salt

Services

Airport

Agriculture

Cattle

Coffee

Orchids

Sugercane

Manufacturing

Textiles

Barranquilla •

• Santa Marta

Cartagena •

• Montería

• Cúcuta

• Bucaramanga

Medellín

• Tunja

Manizales •

• Pereira

BOGOTÁ

• Ibague

• Villavicencio

Buenaventura •

Capital
District

Cali •

• Popayán

• Tumaco

• Buenos Aires

ABOUT THE ECONOMY

GDP
US$245.1 billion (1999). Agriculture 19 percent, industry 26 percent, and services 55 percent.

TERRITORY
Land: 401,044 square miles (1,038,700 square km)
Water: 38,691 square miles (100,210 square km)
Total: 439,736 square miles (1,138,910 square km)

AGRICULTURAL PRODUCTS
Coffee, freshly cut flowers, bananas, sugarcane, cotton, rice, tobacco, and corn.

LABOR FORCE
16.8 million (1997).

UNEMPLOYMENT RATE
20 percent (1999)

INFLATION RATE
9.2 percent (1999)

ENERGY CONSUMPTION PER CAPITA
Equivalent of 606 kilograms of oil (1990-1999)

CURRENCY
Peso (1 peso = 100 centavos)
US$1 = 1,925.63 peso (Jan 2000)

TELEPHONES
Main lines: 5,433,565 (Dec 1997)
Mobile cellular: 1,800,229 (Dec 1998)

RADIOS
21 million (1997)

TELEVISIONS
4.59 million (1997)

INTERNET SERVICE PROVIDERS (ISPS)
13 (1999)

MOTOR VEHICLES
29 per 1,000 inhabitants

PORTS AND HARBORS
Bahia de Portete, Barranquilla, Buenaventura, Cartagena, Leticia, Puerto Bolivar, San Andres, Santa Marta, Tumaco, and Turbo.

MAIN EXPORTS
Oil and oil by-products, coffee, coal, gold, nickel, bananas, flowers, sugar, cotton, gems, textiles, and leather goods.

MAIN IMPORTS
Agricultural machinery, industrial goods, computers, and chemicals.

MAJOR TRADING PARTNERS
United States, Germany, Venezuela, Japan, France, and Brazil.

CULTURAL COLOMBIA

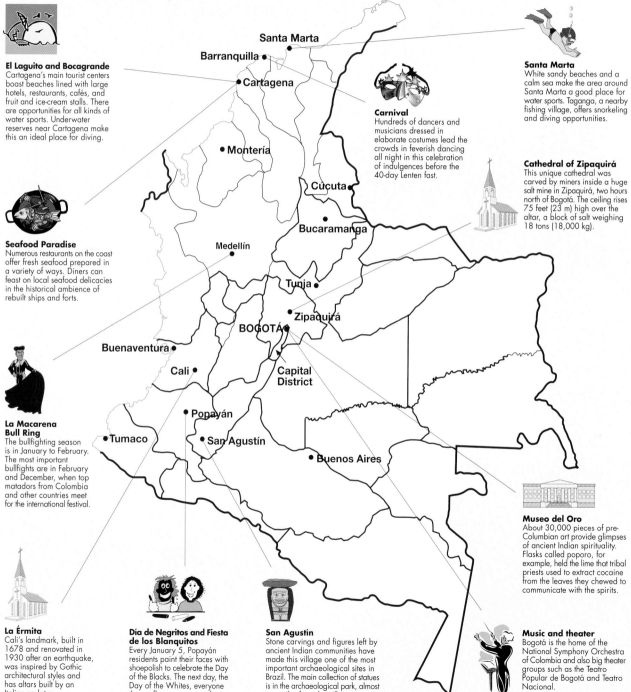

El Laguito and Bocagrande
Cartagena's main tourist centers boast beaches lined with large hotels, restaurants, cafés, and fruit and ice-cream stalls. There are opportunities for all kinds of water sports. Underwater reserves near Cartagena make this an ideal place for diving.

Seafood Paradise
Numerous restaurants on the coast offer fresh seafood prepared in a variety of ways. Diners can feast on local seafood delicacies in the historical ambience of rebuilt ships and forts.

La Macarena Bull Ring
The bullfighting season is in January to February. The most important bullfights are in February and December, when top matadors from Colombia and other countries meet for the international festival.

La Érmita
Cali's landmark, built in 1678 and renovated in 1930 after an earthquake, was inspired by Gothic architectural styles and has altars built by an Italian sculptor.

Día de Negritos and Fiesta de los Blanquitos
Every January 5, Popayán residents paint their faces with shoepolish to celebrate the Day of the Blacks. The next day, the Day of the Whites, everyone throws flour on one another.

San Agustín
Stone carvings and figures left by ancient Indian communities have made this village one of the most important archaeological sites in Brazil. The main collection of statues is in the archaeological park, almost two miles from the village.

Carnival
Hundreds of dancers and musicians dressed in elaborate costumes lead the crowds in feverish dancing all night in this celebration of indulgences before the 40-day Lenten fast.

Santa Marta
White sandy beaches and a calm sea make the area around Santa Marta a good place for water sports. Taganga, a nearby fishing village, offers snorkeling and diving opportunities.

Cathedral of Zipaquirá
This unique cathedral was carved by miners inside a huge salt mine in Zipaquirá, two hours north of Bogotá. The ceiling rises 75 feet (23 m) high over the altar, a block of salt weighing 18 tons (18,000 kg).

Museo del Oro
About 30,000 pieces of pre-Columbian art provide glimpses of ancient Indian spirituality. Flasks called poporo, for example, held the lime that tribal priests used to extract cocaine from the leaves they chewed to communicate with the spirits.

Music and theater
Bogotá is the home of the National Symphony Orchestra of Colombia and also big theater groups such as the Teatro Popular de Bogotá and Teatro Nacional.

Santa Marta
Barranquilla
Cartagena
Montería
Cúcuta
Bucaramanga
Medellín
Tunja
Zipaquirá
BOGOTÁ
Buenaventura
Cali
Capital District
Popayán
Tumaco
San Agustín
Buenos Aires

ABOUT THE CULTURE

OFFICIAL NAME
República de Colombia (Republic of Colombia)

CAPITAL
Santa Fe de Bogotá

DEPARTMENTS (STATES)
Amazonas, Antioquia, Arauca, Atlántico, Bolívar, Boyacá, Caldas, Caquetá, Casanare, Cauca, César, Chocó, Córdoba, Cundinamarca, Guainía, Guaviare, Huila, La Guajira, Magdalena, Meta, Nariño, Norte de Santander, Putumayo, Quindío, Risaralda, San Andrés y Providencia, Santander, Sucre, Tolima, Valle del Cauca, Vaupés, Vichada.

DESCRIPTION OF FLAG
Three horizontal stripes. Yellow stands for Colombia; red for the blood shed for freedom from Spain; and blue for the ocean separating Colombia from Spain.

POPULATION
39,685,655 (2000)

LIFE EXPECTANCY
70 years (2000)

ETHNIC GROUPS
Mixed Spanish and indigenous 58 percent, Caucasian 20 percent, mixed African and Caucasian 14 percent, African 4 percent, mixed indigenous and African 3 percent, and indigenous 1 percent.

MAJOR LANGUAGES
Spanish is the official language. Some Indian groups speak their own languages. The San Andrés and Providencia Islanders speak English.

MAJOR RELIGION
Roman Catholicism 95 percent.

LEADERS IN POLITICS
Bolívar, Simón (1763–1830)—liberator of the Spanish colonies, first president of Gran Colombia. Santander, Francisco de Paula (1792–1840)—Bolívar's right-hand man during the struggle for independence, first elected president of Colombia.

GOVERNMENT SYSTEM
A bicameral Congress, with a 102-seat Senate and 161-seat Chamber of Representatives.

HOLIDAYS
New Year (Jan 1), Epiphany (Jan 6), Saint Joseph's Day (Mar 19), Easter, Labor Day (May 1), Feast of Saints Peter and Paul (Jun 26), Independence Day (Jul 20), Battle of Boyacá (Aug 7), Assumption Day (Aug 15), Día de la Raza (Oct 12), All Saints' Day (Nov 1), Independence of Cartagena (Nov 11), and Christmas (Dec 25). The towns and cities also have their own annual festivals.

TIME LINE

IN COLOMBIA	IN THE WORLD
	753 B.C. Rome is founded.
	116–17 B.C. The Roman Empire reaches its greatest extent, under Emperor Trajan (98-17).
A.D. 200s The Chibchas farm, mine salt and emeralds, and trade with other peoples in the central Andes. They craft pottery, gold works, and cotton fabrics.	
A.D. 400s The Tairona build great stone cities in the Caribbean coastal region.	**A.D. 600** Height of Mayan civilization
	1000 The Chinese perfect gunpowder and begin to use it in warfare.
1499 Alonso de Ojeda meets Amerindians with gold ornaments.	
1533 Pedro de Heredia founds Cartagena. The town becomes Colombia's main trading center and port.	**1530** Beginning of trans-Atlantic slave trade organized by the Portuguese in Africa.
1536 The Spanish found Bogotá and Cali.	**1558–1603** Reign of Elizabeth I of England
	1620 Pilgrim Fathers sail the Mayflower to America.
1717 The Spanish create the Viceroyalty of New Granada to administer Colombia, Venezuela, and Ecuador.	**1776** U.S. Declaration of Independence
1781 A tax rebellion becomes the first Colombian revolt against Spanish power.	**1789–1799** The French Revolution
1808 Napoleon Bonaparte takes over the Spanish crown and gives it to his brother Joseph. Many Spanish colonies refuse to recognize Joseph as their ruler.	
1819 Simón Bolívar ousts the Spanish and establishes the republic of Gran Colombia.	**1861** The U.S. Civil War begins.

IN COLOMBIA	IN THE WORLD
1830 Bolívar dies. Ecuador and Venezuela gain independence. Colombia becomes the Republic of New Granada.	**1869** The Suez Canal is opened. **1914** World War I begins. **1939** World War II begins. **1945** The United States drops atomic bombs on Hiroshima and Nagasaki.
1948 *La Violencia* ("The Violence") erupts.	**1949** The North Atlantic Treaty Organization (NATO) is formed.
1957 Women win the right to vote. The Liberal and Conservative parties form the National Front and alternate presidency for the next 16 years.	**1957** The Russians launch Sputnik.
1974 The National Front agreement is extended for another 17 years.	**1966–1969** The Chinese Cultural Revolution
1980s Rise of the *Narcotraficantes*, or druglords.	
1985 Guerrilla group M-19 occupies the Palace of Justice. Their battle with the military kills over 100 people.	**1986** Nuclear power disaster at Chernobyl in Ukraine **1991** Break-up of the Soviet Union
1993 The most famous druglord, Pablo Escobar, is killed.	**1997** Hong Kong is returned to China.
1999 An earthquake in Armenia, western Colombia, kills at least 1,185 people, injures more than 4,750, and leaves about 250,000 homeless.	
2000 U.S. President Bill Clinton approves Plan Colombia to stop rural drug production.	**2001** World population surpasses 6 billion.

GLOSSARY

bogotano ("bog-o-TAN-no")
Belonging to Bogotá; an inhabitant of Bogotá.

compadrazgo ("kom-pah-DRAHS-go")
The spiritual relationship between a child's godparents and parents.

cartel
A group of manufacturers colluding to control the supply of a good so as to control prices.

colegios ("co-LAY-he-os")
Schools.

conquistador ("kon-KEES-tah-dor")
A 16th-century Spanish conqueror.

cordillera ("kor-deel-LYAH-rah")
A mountain range.

department
What a state is called in Colombia.

El Dorado
The mythical city rumored to abound in gold.

escuelas ("es-coo-AY-las")
Schools.

feria ("FAY-re-ah")
A festival associated with a religious pilgrimage.

llanos ("LYAH-nos")
Grassy lowlands.

matador ("mah-tah-DOR")
The bullfighter who kills the bull.

mestizo ("mes-TEE-soh")
Someone of Spanish-Indian ancestry.

plaza de toros ("PLAH-sah de TOH-ros")
A bullfighting ring.

sabana ("sah-BAH-nah")
A treeless plain, or savannah.

tambos ("TAM-bos")
A bamboo or thatched house built on stilts.

tejo ("TAY-ho")
A traditional game resembling horseshoes.

tienda ("te-EN-dah")
A small neighborhood shop.

vaquero ("vah-KAY-ro")
A Colombian cowboy.

FURTHER INFORMATION

BOOKS

Bergquist, C. (editor), et al. *Violence in Colombia 1990–2000. Waging War and Negotiating Peace (Latin American Silhouettes)*. Wilmington: Scholarly Resources, 2001.

Bushnell, D. and Georg Wilhelm Friedrich Hegel. *The Making of Modern Colombia: A Nation in Spite of Itself*. California: University of California Press, 1993.

Metaxas, Eric and Diana Bryan. *The Monkey People: A Colombian Folktale*. New York: Simon & Schuster, 1995.

Villegas, Benjamin. *The Taste of Colombia*. New York: St. Martin's Press, 1997.

von Rothkirch, Cristobal. *Alta Colombia: The Splendor of the Mountains*. New York: St. Martin's Press, 1997.

WEBSITES

Central Intelligence Agency World Factbook (select "Colombia" from the country list).
www.odci.gov/cia/publications/factbook/index.html

Colombia Support Network. www.colombiasupport.net

Colombia Update. www.colombiaupdate.com

Global Exchange Colombia Campaign. www.globalexchange.org/colombia

Learning Network reference (type "Colombia" in the search box). http://ln.infoplease.com

Lonely Planet World Guide: Destination Colombia.
www.lonelyplanet.com/destinations/south_america/colombia

MUSIC

Colombia: Nuevas Voces. Sony Music, 1997.

Greatest Cumbia Classics of Colombia. Discos Fuentes, 1997.

Putumayo Presents: Colombia. Putumayo World Music, 2001.

VIDEO

New Horizons For Human Rights. UN Productions, 1991.

BIBLIOGRAPHY

Background Notes: Republic of Colombia. Washington, D.C.: US Department of State. Updated periodically.

Colombia in Pictures. Minneapolis: Lerner Publications Company, 1987.

Labbe, Armand J. *Colombia Before Columbus*. New York: Rizzoli International Publications, Inc., 1986.

INDEX

Afro-Colombians, 51, 56, 57, 95
agriculture, 31, 33
airport, 39
Andean Common Market, 40
Andes, 5, 8, 9, 37, 38, 97
animals, 10
architecture, 17, 94
arts, 5, 87–97
Atlantic Ocean, 57
aviation, 39

Baha'is, 76
bananas, 33, 34, 126
Benalcázar, Sebastian de, 21
biodiversity, 43
body language, 83
bogotanas, 66
Bolívar, Simón, 23, 24, 39, 90
Bolivia, 45
Botero, Fernando, 93

Brazil, 7, 32
Buddhists, 76
bullfighting, 16, 102
business, 68

cafés, 87, 128
Canada, 39
Cannes Film Festival, 97
Caribbean Sea, 7
carnival, 113
cathedrals, 79
Catholic Church, 24, 55, 75, 87
cattle, 13, 35
Cauca Valley, 37, 51, 100
cereal, 61
Chibcha, 19, 20, 52, 64
Chile, 35
cities
    Armero, 13
    Barranquilla, 8, 14, 31, 100,

113
Bogotá, 5, 14, 15, 21, 23, 27,
    28, 34, 35, 37, 38, 39, 52,
    59, 66, 73, 81, 83, 85, 87,
    94, 97
Bucaramanga, 14, 81
Buenaventura, 35, 39
Cali, 14, 16, 17, 21, 37, 39,
    66, 79, 87, 93, 101, 107
Cartagena, 14, 17, 21, 22, 23,
    75, 79, 94, 99, 100
Cúcuta, 14, 23
Ibagué, 14
Leticia, 61
Medellín, 14, 16, 31, 32, 33,
    37, 41, 72, 79, 81, 85, 87
Pasto, 21
Pereira, 14
Popayán, 21, 79, 94, 96
San Agustín, 15, 19

Santa Marta, 14, 21, 38
Tumaco, 35
Tunja, 94
Zipaquirá, 79
climate, 33, 34, 59, 72
cocaine, 16, 41
cockfighting, 104
coffee, 11, 16, 24, 31, 33, 40, 61, 119
Columbus, Christopher, 7
compadre, 64
compadrazgo, 64
conquistadores, 21, 51, 88
congress, 25, 27
constitution, 27, 75, 76
cordilleras, 7, 51
Cordillera Central, 8, 13, 52
Cordillera Occidental, 8
Cordillera Oriental, 8
Creoles, 88
currency, 31

dancing, 107
dating, 65
departments (states)
Antioquia, 22
Chocó, 9, 47, 56, 57, 63
La Guajira, 9
Providencia, 7, 57, 81
San Andrés, 7, 57, 81
Día de Negritos, 110
drama, 97

earthquakes, 17
Ecuador, 7, 21, 22, 23, 39, 45
education, 55, 64, 67, 70
El Dorado, 19, 20, 39
elections, 29
El Libertador, 24
emeralds, 12, 36
environment, 43–49

family, 62, 63, 66, 67, 73, 117
fauna, 10, 46
Federmann, Nicolaus de, 21
ferias, 108
fiesta, 102, 107
Fiesta de los Blanquitos, 110

fishing, 35, 61
flora, 11, 46
flowers, 11, 34
food, 117–131
France, 32
French Revolution, 23
Freyle, Juan Rodríquez, 89

Gaitán, Jorge Eliécer, 25
Germany, 32
gestures, 83
gold, 12, 16, 19, 22, 36, 41
Gorgona, 7
Gorgonilla, 7
Gran Colombia, 23
Great Depression, 25, 31
greetings, 84
Guajira Peninsula, 12, 51
guerrillas, 25

high altitude cooking, 123
Hindus, 76
houses, 17, 72
hydroelectricity, 12

independence, 23, 114
Indians, 19, 21, 53, 95, 96
Isla Fuerte, 7
Islas del Rosario, 7

Japan, 32
journalists, 85
judiciary, 28

La Macarena, 16
La Violencia, 25
literature, 5, 87, 90, 91
llanos, 37, 61, 101

machismo, 66
Malpelo, 7
Manizales, 14
market days, 69
Márquez, Gabriel García, 91
marriage, 65
meat, 61, 117, 120

mestizo, 51, 56
minerals, 36
mining, 36, 54
mulatto, 56
music, 96, 107
Muslims, 76

national parks
Los Estoraques, 46
Los Flamencos, 46
Los Katios, 47
Tairona, 7
National Railway System, 39
natural gas, 12
Nevado del Ruiz, 13
newspapers, 85
novels, 91
Nueva Granada, 21, 22, 23, 89
Nuñez, Raphael, 24

Obregón, Alejandro, 93
Ojeda, Alfonso de, 19

Pacific Ocean, 7
Panama, 7, 23, 24, 47
Pan-American Highway, 39
Peru, 7, 23, 35, 45
petroleum, 12, 24, 31
piranhas, 10
Plan Colombia, 49
plants, 11
Plaza de Bolívar, 15, 79
ports, 22, 35
power plants, 24
private enterprise, 32

Quesada, Gonzalo Jiménez de, 21, 89, 90
Quimbayas, 52

radio, 71, 85
railroads, 24
Rayo Museum, 93
roads, 39
rivers, 10, 12, 37
Amazon River, 8
Atrato River, 8, 47

Catatumbo River, 37
Magdalena River, 8, 21, 35, 37, 38
Orinoco River, 8
Sinú River, 8
ruana, 59

sabana, 34
San Bernardo, 7
San Isidro, 109
Sierra Nevada, 48, 101
slaves, 54
slums, 17, 72
Spanish, 5, 17, 19, 21, 22, 24, 36, 51, 54, 57, 63, 79, 81, 82
sports, 100
    hunting, 101
    mountaineering, 101
    soccer, 104
    water sports, 100
sugarcane, 34

table manners, 123
tejo, 105
television, 71, 85
theater, 97
transportation, 38, 69

unemployment, 15
Unión Patriótica, 25
United States, 24, 27, 32, 39, 40, 41, 48, 51, 57, 66, 94, 117
universities, 71
U'wa, 48

vaqueros, 61
Venezuela, 7, 22, 23, 32, 39, 45
volcanoes, 8
voting, 29

War of a Thousand Days, 24
work week, 68

Yagua, 53